Mountains of the Provençal Rim

Multi-day walks in the Cévennes, Diois Hills, Vercors, Dévoluy, Écrins, Queyras, Chambeyron and Maritime Alps

Ian C M MacLennan

Copyright © 2017 Ian C M MacLennan

All rights reserved.

ISBN-10:1979955646
ISBN-13:9781979955645

DEDICATION

To my walking companions – Pam the three Johns and Andrew

Also by Ian MacLennan

Walking the Alps from Mediterranean to Adriatic
An account of a complete traverse of the Alps from Menton on the Côte d'Azure to Vittorio Veneto at the edge of the Venetian plain

Amazon 2014

CONTENTS

		Acknowledgments	i
1	Chapter —	Discovering the Southern Hills	Pg 1
2	Chapter —	From the Vercors to the Queyras Alps	Pg 5
3	Chapter —	Gorges and watersheds of the Cévennes	Pg 37
4	Chapter —	High ridges of the Diois Hills	Pg 77
5	Chapter —	Escarpments of the Dévoluy and Vercors	Pg 97
6	Chapter —	Crêtes and baisses of the Alpes Maritimes	Pg 127
7	Chapter —	Traverse of the border alps from the coast	Pg 141
8	Chapter —	High passes of the Southern Écrins	Pg 173
9	Appendices		Pg 193

      i. When to walk
      ii. Mapping
      iii. Estimated times for each day's walk
      iv. Finding and booking accommodation
      v. Equipment

| 10 | Index | | Pg 197 |

ACKNOWLEDGMENTS

Firstly I thank my walking companions. John Simmons, John Delamere, John Milles, my wife Pam and my son Andrew. They joined me on many of the walks. Their companionship enormously increased the enjoyment of these adventures. I also thank them for kindly allowing me to use some of their photographs in this book.

I am indebted to John Delamere and my wife Pam for proof reading the manuscript and for many helpful suggestions.

Digital IGN 1:25k maps supplied by Memorymap www.memory-map.co.uk with the memorymap software have been used in planning and undertaking these walks. Details of these are given in the appendix to this book. Recently I have made extensive use of the IGN maps that are accessible free on the Geoportail Website: https://www.geoportail.gouv.fr.

Amazon CreateSpace https://www.createspace.com/Products/Book/ have enabled me to convert the manuscript describing my walks into a publishable and published book. I am most grateful for the helpful and efficient service they have provided.

Finally I would like to thank all the wonderful people who welcomed and fed us and provided accommodation each night on these multi-day walks.

ICMM December 2017

1 CHAPTER
DISCOVERING THE SOUTHERN HILLS

On a misty morning at the start of May 1979 my heavily laden Morris Minor toiled up the road from le Puy to the plateau of the Haute Loire. On reaching the high pastures the mist was below and the engine began to sing as we crossed the plateau. Drifts of pale yellow appeared in the green grass. They looked like daffodils. I slowed. They were daffodils, stretching towards the skyline. These floral alps of the Haute Loire were the first of the groups of Southern French hills to seduce me. Since then my passion has continued to grow for the highlands that rise within Provence and on the outer rim of this region of southeastern France.

The journey across the Haute Loire was the start of sabbatical leave from Oxford, when I was to engage in research in the newly-formed Centre d'Immunologie de Marseille Luminy. This sabbatical in the south of France proved life-changing in terms of my academic career and also gave me months to roam free and explore the hills of the region.

This book describes seven multi-day walks, through the impressive series of southern French hills that border on the outer rim of Provence. These walks are summarized in the map on page 3. The 72 days of walks described in this book cover a series of eight mountain ranges. Rising on the west side of the Rhône are the green hills of the Cévennes, while on the Rhône's eastern side and in northern Provence lie the Diois Hills. To the north of these hills are the high cliffs that defend the Vercors plateau. Moving further east from this plateau is a ring of sharp limestone peaks that form the Dévoluy and these are separated from the truly alpine Écrins Massive by the river Drac. Continuing east from the Écrins and across the River Durance lie the border hills. From north to south these are the Queyras, Chambeyron and Maritime Alps.

All of these walks were undertaken with from one to three companions The start of the walks are generally accessible by public transport and finish at places where a bus or train is available to return home. Each day's walk ends at a mountain refuge, a gîte d'étape or a hotel. The lodgings used always provide an evening meal and breakfast, so it is only necessary to carry food and water for the day. Enough detail is given to allow the reader to follow these routes and to convey the joy of these long walks through the mountains on the rim of Provence.

Dandelions in May in the Dévoluy with the western escarpment in the background

Discovering the southern hills

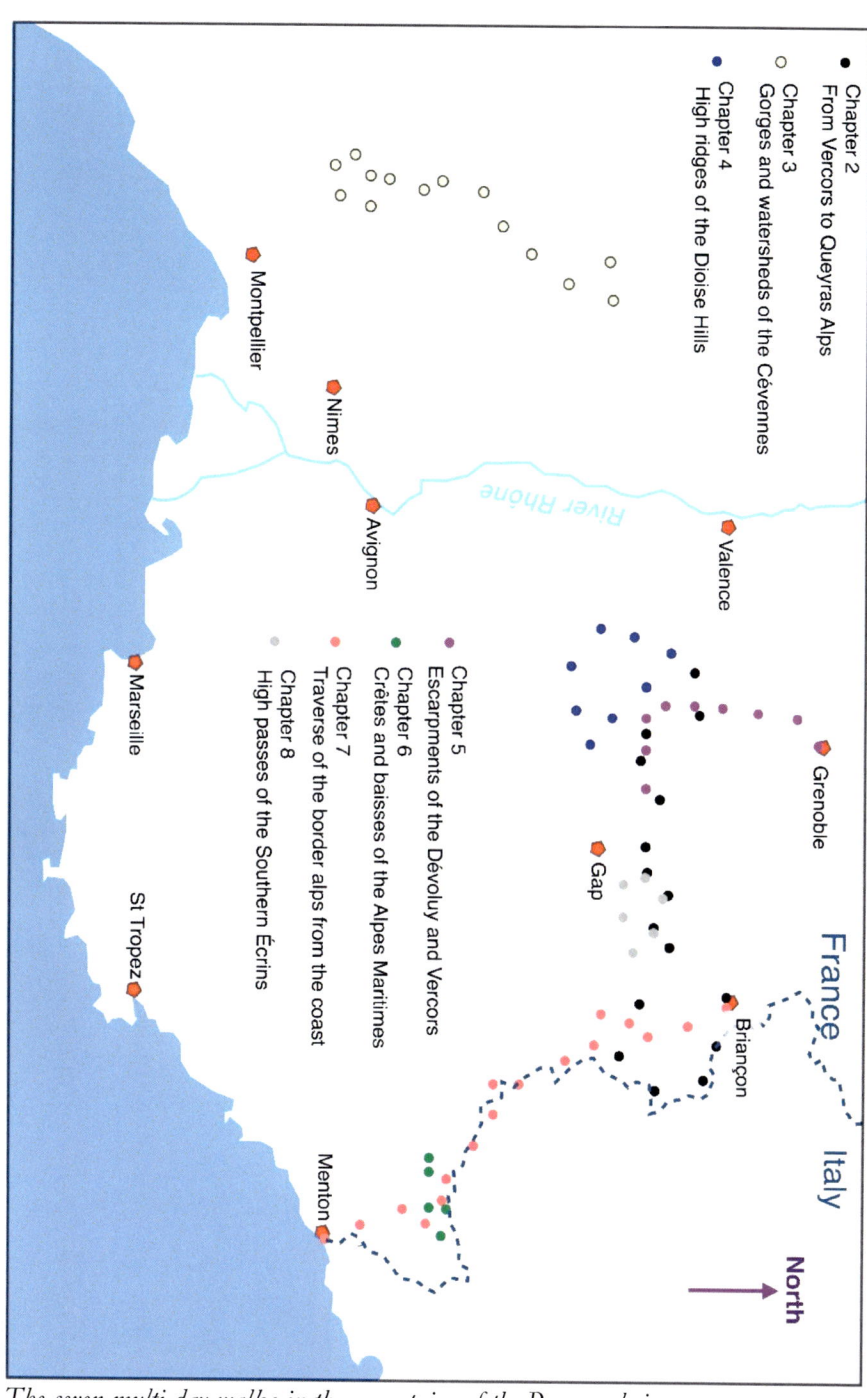

The seven multi-day walks in the mountains of the Provençal rim

Summary of the seven walks in the Mountains of the Provençal Rim

Chapter 2: From the Vercors to the Queyras Alps:
a 15 day walk from Die to Briançon
Total distance 299km, ascent 19,948m, daily average 19.9km, with 1,332m ascent

Chapter 3: Gorges and watersheds of the Cévennes:
a 12 day walk from Cazilhac to la Bastide Puylaurent.
Total distance 248.7km, ascent 12,596m, daily average 20.7km, 1049m ascent

Chapter 4: High ridges of the Diois Hills:
an 8 day circular walk from Die.
Total distance, 161.6km, ascent 10,294m; total average 20.2km, 1,287m ascent

Chapter 5: Escarpments of the Dévoluy and Vercors:
a 9 day walk from Lus-la-Croix-Haute to Grenoble
Total distance 167km, ascent 11,605m, daily average 18.6km, 1,289m ascent

Chapter 6: Crêtes and baisses of the Alpes Maritimes:
a 6 day circular walk from St-Martin-Vesubie
Total distance 109km, ascent 9,447m, daily average 18.2km, 1,575m ascent

Chapter 7: Traverse of the border alps from the coast:
a 15 day walk from Menton to Briançon
Total distance 262.6km, ascent 22,619m, daily average 17.5km, 1,508m ascent

Chapter 8: High passes of the Southern Écrins:
two and five day circular walks from les Borels
Total distance 116.9km, ascent 8,591m, daily average 16.7km, 1,227m ascent

The total of all walks is 1,365km covered in 72 days with 95,100m ascent, giving a daily average of 19km with 1,321m ascent

2 CHAPTER
FROM THE VERCORS TO THE QUEYRAS ALPS
A 15 day walk from Die to Briançon of 299km with 19,948m ascent

A series of four mountain ranges lie between Valance on the Rhône and the Italian border. First the high limestone cliffs of the Vercors defend an immense and varied plateau some 1,500 to 2,000m high. The east edge of the plateau rises to a long and impressive line of rocky peaks that fall precipitously on their eastern flank to the pass between Grenoble and Sisteron. Beyond lies the Dévoluy; a ring of sharp limestone mountains of 65km circumference that surrounds exquisite green pastures (photographed on page 2). On the eastern side of the Dévoluy runs the river Drac and beyond this is the Écrins Massif. These are serious mountains with the high point the Barre des Écrins reaching 4102m. Finally to the east of the Écrins the beautiful Queyras Alps extend to the border ridge between France and Italy with the outlier Monte Viso standing at 3841m beyond the southwestern corner of these high hills.

The traverse of these four ranges described here starts from Die in the Drôme Valley with an immediate ascent of the massive limestone cliffs that guard the southern edge of the Vercors plateau. On the far side of the convoluted wilderness of the plateau an equally abrupt descent leads to a quirky château near the foot of the rock tower of Mont Aiguille. During the following two days the route follows a ridge southwards from the southeastern corner of the Vercors plateau before descending to the hidden valley that guards the headwaters of the River Buëch. The escape from this valley is by a high pass that breaches the limestone ridge guarding the verdant centre of the Dévoluy. After spending a night in St Disdier in the Dévoluy the walk passes through a gap in the eastern side of the chain of peaks and then makes a long curved descent to the Drac valley. Following a night at St Bonnet en Champsaur, it takes four marvellous days to traverse the southern hills of the Écrins before crossing the River Durance and climbing into the Queyras. Another five days walking in a spectacular semicircle close to and at times along and the frontier ridge ends with a descent to the ancient frontier town of Briançon. This 15-day walk was undertaken at the end of June 2007.

The Écrins from the Northern Queyras Ridge: Day14

Stages of the walk from Die to Briançon

Day 1 – Die, Ferme des Chazeaux (750m) to Chichilianne (977m)
18.0 km, up 1,338m, down 1,141m, high point Cabane de Chaumailloux 1,669m, 6h27

Day 2 – Chichilianne to Grimone (1,140m)
20.4 km, up 1,674m, down 1,534m high point the summit of the Jocou 2,051m 7h43

Day 3 – Grimone to la Jarjatte (1,176m)
18.1 km, up 1,283m, down 1,229m, high point summit of the Aupillon 1,744m, 6h25

Day 4 – la Jarjatte to St-Disdier (1,040m)
18.5 km, up 1,265m, down 1,383m, high point Col de Charnier 2,103m, 6h33

Day 5 – St-Disdier to St-Bonnet-en-Champsaur (1,023m)
28.4 km, up 1,655m, down 1,697m, high point the Col la Saume 1,704m, 9h22

Day 6 – St-Bonnet-en-Champsaur to Chaillol (1,455m)
21.8km, up 1,735m, down 1,307m, high point the Barry 2,271m, 7h57

Day 7 – Chaillol to les Gondoins (1,311m)
18.3 km, up 1,418m, down 1,532m, high point Aiguilles du Pertuis 1,850m, 6h52

Day 8 – les Gondoins to Prapic (1,590m)
19.5 km, up 973m, down 725m, high point at Girardet 1,650 m, 5h55

Day 9 – Prapic to Dormillouse (1,681m)
17.9 km, up 1,334m, down 1,185m, high point the Col des Fressinières 2,782 m, 6h27

Day 10 – Dormillouse to Guillestre (1,007m)
26.0 km, up 749m, 1,446m down, high point at the start at 1,681m, 7h14

Day 11 – Pied du Mélezet (1,702m) to Maljasset (1,910m)
12.1 km, up 1,130m, 943m down, high point the Col Girardin 2,695m, 4h48

Day 12 – Maljasset to Refuge Agnel (2,580m)
18.6km, up 1,578m, down 917, high point Col de la Noire 2,955m, 6h50

Day 13 – Refuge Agnel to le Roux (1,735m)
21.9 km, up 1,427m, 2,267m down, high point Col Vieux 2,806m, 8h00

Day 14 – le Roux to les Fonts (2,040m)
14.8 km, up 1,494m, 1,201m down, high point 2,921m Col de Rasis, 6h06

Day 15 – les Fonts to Briançon (1,212m)
25.0 km, up 895m, 1,727m down, high point 2,204m Bergerie de Peyre Moutte, 7h26

Total distance 299km, total ascent 19,948m

Daily average 19.9km, with 1,332m ascent

Mountains of the Provençal Rim

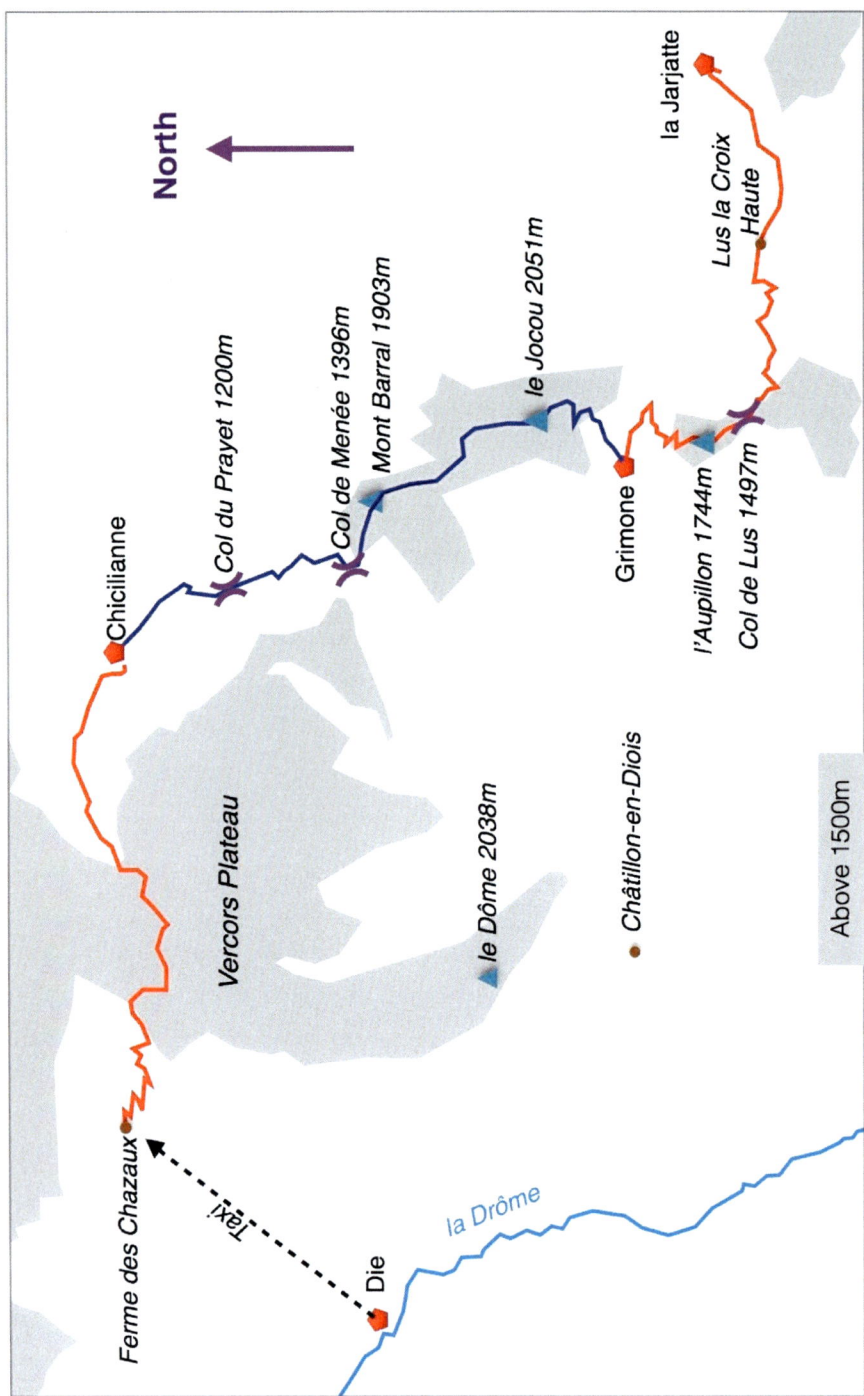

Across the Vercors from Die to la Jarjatte

21/5/2018

Dear Sara,

Very many thanks for organising such a super reunion.

The venue was perfect, great fun punting, amazing city tours on foot and bus and best of all 'catching up' with good friends.

I don't know if you have 'walked' in France, if not perhaps you will find Ian's book tempting to go. We are returning to our favourite places there next week for 'gentle' walking.

I did not do any of the walks in the book!

Love Pam.

The journey to Die (396m)

The name of this ancient town is pronounced "Dee", so it doesn't sound so ominous as it looks when you write to your friends telling them you are going to Die. Trains run to Die from Lyon, Valance and Gap. The train from Valance goes down the east bank of the Rhône before turning east and groaning its way up the Drôme valley. As it approaches Die, the cliffs of the Vercors Escarpment come into view rising some 1,600m behind the town. La Petite Auberge http://www.lapetiteauberge-traiteur.com lies just across the road from the station and provides convenient, comfortable accommodation with meals at affordable prices.

View from the balcony path on the Southern Vercors Escarpment past the Dent de Die

Day 1: Ferme des Chazeau (750m) to Chichilianne (977m)
18.0 km, up 1,338m, down 1,141m high point Cabane de Chaumailloux 1,669m, 6h27

It is a pleasant enough 9km from Die up the Meyrosse Valley on the D742, or the parallel footpath, to the Ancienne Ferme des Chazeau. Heavy rain overnight and during the morning, with the promise of a fine afternoon, persuaded the author to omit this road section and take a taxi to the point where the valley road becomes a route forestière. From there the once-metaled lane winds its way up the east side of the valley gaining some 300m in 3.5km. Then it reaches a modern, locked shelter, marked on the IGN 1:25k map as "le Château", but this is no castle. The steep path leading to the plateau, marked with yellow and brown way-marks, starts behind the shelter. The path climbs in short zigzags through scrub gaining 450m in 0.6km before joining a balcony path. Contouring on this path north-westwards, below the lip of the escarpment there are fine views back towards Die (above). Ahead rises the summit ridge of the Grand

Veymont, the highest peak in the Vercors[1]. After a little over a km the path reaches a breach in the escarpment lip and turns right past another shelter. It soon emerges from the woods and continues up a grassy hollow before levelling off and joining Grande Radonnée (GR) 91/93. This footpath runs southwards on the plateau. Shortly after the Col du Pison the route leaves the GR, heading just north of east on a path, marked with black dashes on the map that leads towards the Bergerie du Jas Neuf. This flower-filled grassland is studded with a maze of limestone outcrops and hollows that make it important to pay attention to navigation. Just before the bergerie a turn south leads to a path that runs north-eastwards some distance in the front of the buildings. Soon the distinctive profile of Mont Aiguille comes into view (below) and dominates the way ahead. This striking peak has a flat grassy summit that is cut off from access on all sides by impressive cliffs. In 1492 this was a site of pioneering rock climbing, when King Charles VIII of France challenged Antoine de Ville to climb the aiguille. De Ville took up the challenge and with a team of helpers, ladders and other artificial aids, reached the summit and returned safely.

Mont Aiguille from the top of the pass de l'Aiguille

Some way after the bergerie the path curves round to the east and just before reaching the octagonal Cabane de Chaumailloux the route turns to the north. The path then passes to the left of a small tarn and after this the graves of 8 members of the resistance, killed in these hills during the second world war. Now, at the Pas de l'Aiguille, the path falls steeply to the left of a stream that forms a striking waterfall cascading from the plateau. Towards the base of the escarpment the path passes through woods and, as the gradient eases, joins

---

[1] The ascent of this ridge of the Grand Veymont is described in Chapter 4 in the account of Day 6 of the walk from Lus-la-Croix-Haute to Grenoble

a white stony track. This leads across open fields to the hamlet of Richardière, which lies at the base of Mont Aiguille. At the end of this hamlet a right turn (south) on the D7b crosses a bridge and continues for 3km to Chichilianne. In the centre of the village a turn to the east leads to the Château de Passières http://www.chateau-de-passieres.fr.cx, marked 'chât' on the map. This is an interesting stopover. The ground floor rooms and the stone spiral staircase have their walls hung with an extraordinary mixture of paintings. The number of pictures that cram the walls does not give the greatest artistic effect. Nevertheless, there are some interesting and fine works, including paintings by the French mid-20th century artist, Edith Berger, who worked in this region.

Rustic water troughs on the way to the Col du Prayet

Day 2 – Chichilianne to Grimone (1,140m)
20.4 km, up 1,674m, down 1,534m high point: the Jocou summit 2,051m 7h43

The lane that heads eastwards from the château soon joins the D7 road. Then a right turn leads south-south-eastwards towards the Col du Prayet. Half a km up the road the route follows a broad stony path to the left that climbs through woods, passing a series of rustic water troughs hollowed out of tree trunks (above). This path later becomes a track that passes the Bergerie des Ayes and continues southwards to the Col du Prayet. Looking back from the col is a fine view of Mont Aiguille and the eastern escarpment of the Vercors. On the far side of the col the route to the Col de Menée is quite complex. This begins with a steep descent through woods on a track and then a path. After the path winds round to the left a left fork is taken. This passes the track leading to the remains of the Ermitage d'Esparron before joining a forestry road. The road is followed to the right across a bridge and then uphill. It then goes through a hairpin bend, as it passes the Ferme d'Esparron before splitting into two tracks. The route follows the left fork southeastwards uphill and takes the right branch at two subsequent forks before reaching another track. Turning right onto this the walk continues south-eastwards climbing to a route forestière that traverses southwards for 0.5km. Then a stony path is followed to the left that climbs clockwise round a forested cirque to the narrow D7 road that runs from Clelles in the Trièves to Châtillion-en-Diois. Our route continues to follow the path on the far side of the road and soon reaches the Col de Menée, while the road passes through a tunnel beneath the col. The col itself is grassy and covered with flowers in early summer, with a large wooden cross standing on its western side. The way forward is on a path that leads just south of east towards Mont Barral. The path soon becomes a steep climb up a broad grassy ridge topped by a sharp limestone summit ridge, from which there are magnificent views.

The Eastern Vercors escarpment from the north summit of the Jocou

The descent from Mont Barral on the steep south ridge has some exposure, but is interesting rather than dangerous. It leads to the Crête de Jiboui, a largely level, but sharp-sided grassy ridge that runs southwards for some 3 km. At the low point of the crête GR 93 joins from the right and continues along the crête to the Col de Seysse. There the main GR93 goes straight ahead traversing on the western flank of the last and highest hill on the ridge, the Jocou. The preferred route climbs left on a GR93 variant. When the variant path reaches a grass-patched limestone buttress there is a scramble up this southwards to the north summit of the Jocou. The view back (above) looks past Mont Barral with the Eastern Vercors escarpment stretching away to the north. The summit of the already-distant Mont Aiguille is crowned by the Grand Veymont. To the west are the tops of the cliffs above Die, while the high hills of the Écrins and Dévoluy dominate the view to the east. The main summit of the Jocou lies to the south and is reached by an grassy ridge. The route continues southwards from this summit on the variant GR and, after entering sparse woodland, descends in zigzags. At la Pouyat, GR93 variant rejoins the GR93, which heads south to the Col de Grimone, our route descends south-westwards on a path through meadows to Grimone itself. On the descent the path twice crosses the zigzagging D539 on the way to this village. The Gîte-La Sauvagine http://gite-lasauvagine.fr, lying above the road in the village, is a good stopover.

The Western Dévoluy Escarpment from the south end of the Aupillon ridge

Day 3: Grimone to La Jarjatte (1,176m)
18.1 km, up 1,283m, down 1,229m, high point Aupillon summit 1,744m, 6h25

From the road just east of the village a track descends to the right, crosses a stream and then leads up through floral fields directly to the Col de Grimone. The route then turns back to the west on a track, before taking the second of two paths to the left, following signs to l'Aupillon and the Col de Lus. This path is way-marked with yellow and green flashes and at first contours westwards through woods high above Grimone. Eventually the path loops back to the east and comes out onto open steep hillside. After another loop the path crosses the northwest ridge of the Serre les Têtes and then traverses south-eastwards to the grassy Col des Prêtres. A sign there indicates the way from this col to the summit of l'Aupillon. The ridge over this craggy hill offers fine views to the eastern escarpment of the Dévoluy (above). Eventually the high ridge ends and falls sharply to the Col de Lus, where there is a crossing of paths and tracks. The route follows the path, labelled as the Chemin des Templiers on the map. This runs south-eastwards from the col through forest and is marked with red mountain bike signs and occasional red and yellow flashes. At one point the cycle way-mark is accompanied by a danger sign, which is justified, for on turning the next corner the path ends abruptly and a steep rocky slab leads down to a torrent. On the far side, the path continues to traverse across steep wooded hillside to the open grassy Col Navite. From this col the route continues on the Chemin des Templiers, descending across open ground south-eastwards and then to the east. After entering more woods, a shallow stream and the path share the same ground for a few yards. Then the waters fall to the right and the path continues through a grove of box. Soon there is a sign indicating that the Chemin des Templiers doubles back to the right, but our route continues straight ahead, following signs to Lus. This path contours round a southeast-facing cirque and on the far side passes the ruins of a farm. It then winds down through forest. At a splitting of the path the left fork leads to a lane that winds down to the Gap-Grenoble railway and main Grenoble-Sisteron road at la Meyrie. On the far side of the road the route passes through a garage forecourt and crosses two footbridges. It then follows a path, not marked on the current IGN map, which leads through hayfields to Lus-la-Croix-Haute.

The aiguilles to the south of la Jarjatte

It is a pleasant 5.5km walk from Lus along the D505 to la Jarjatte. This passes through meadows and then goes through a gap in the hills to the hidden valley of the Buëch headwaters. Just after the D505 crosses the river, a lane forking to the right leads into la Jarjatte. Above the village there is a cirque that is headed by the impressive rocky peaks of the Tête de la Garnisier, the Tête de la Plainie and the Haute Bouffet. (The 'photo above shows these peaks in the evening sunset)[2]. Turning right then left and right again in the village leads to the modern comfortable and welcoming Gîte d'Étape la Jarjatte-Valgabondage +33 4 92 58 52 88. This provides meals and twin rooms with their own shower and toilet.

Day 4 – La Jarjatte to St Disdier (1,040m)
18.5 km, up 1,265m, down 1,383m, high point Col de Charnier 2,103m, 6h33

The walk follows the GR93 across the western escarpment of the Dévoluy and reverses part of the walk of Day 2 described in Chapter 4. Although the distance is not great, the way to the Col de Charnier is steep and committing.

---

[2] A walk across these jagged peaks is described in Chapter 4, Day 1.

From Vercors to the Queyras Alps

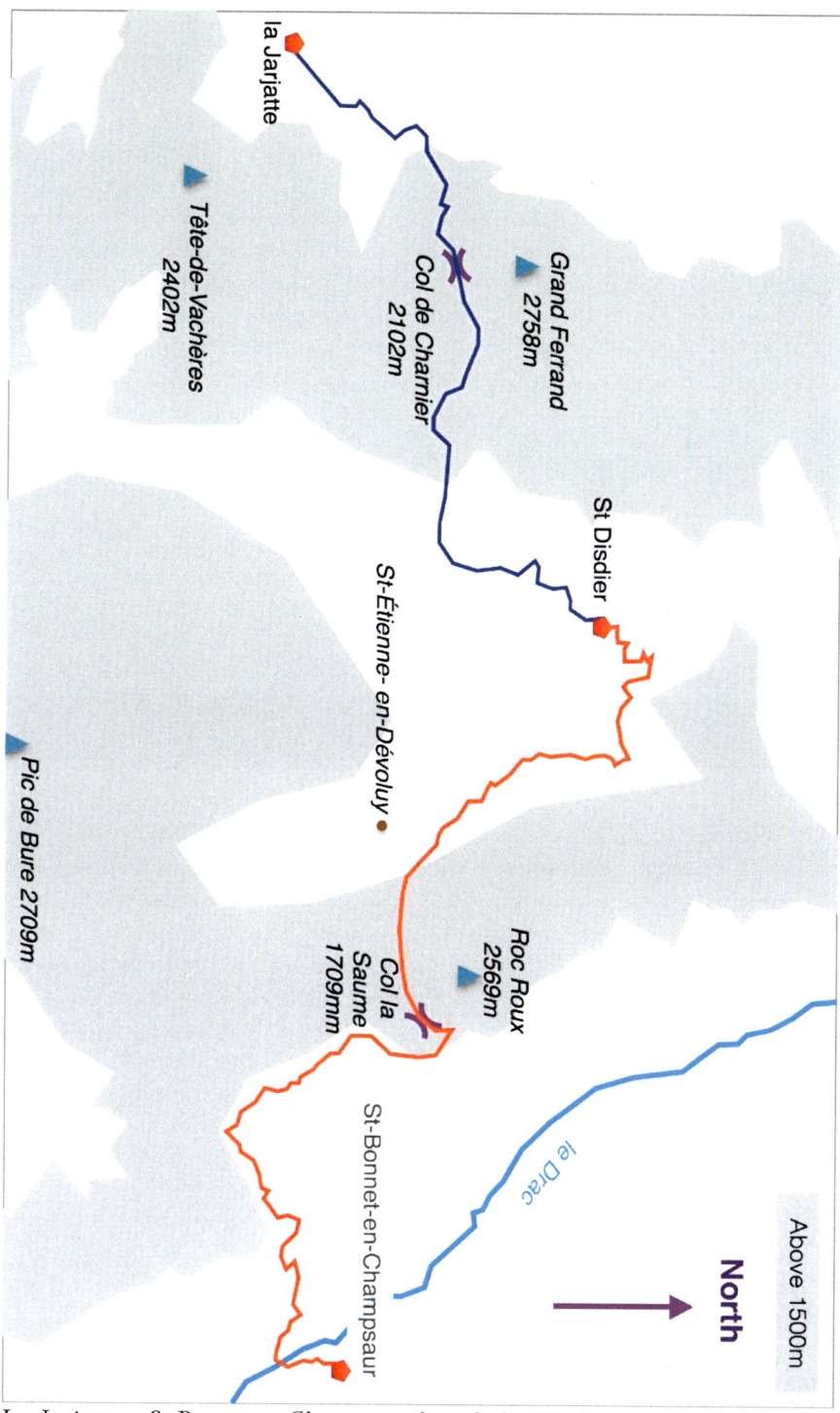

La Jarjatte to St-Bonnet-en-Champsaur through the Dévoluy

The walk heads northeastwards on the D505 lane up the valley following the south bank of the Buëch. After 2km the lane crosses the river and half a km after the bridge a track is followed to the left that climbs to the Col de la Croix (the low point to the left in the ridge in the photo below). Here the route joins up with GR93.

From the col the GR is followed to the right, at first to the north of the grassy ridge leading up to the Tête de Lauzon (seen below as the central peak with the rocky summit). The path then briefly follows the ridge before making a steep diagonal across the grassy south face, eventually reaching a line of limestone that forms the rim of a hidden hanging valley below the main cliffs. This lonely but exhilarating place encircles a small tarn and is backed by the massive white summit cliffs. After passing to the left of the tarn there is a steep climb up scree and rocks to the Col de Charnier.

The Tête de Lauzon from the Buëch headwaters

From the col it is a pleasant walk down the verdant Charnier valley, with views of the snowy peaks of the Écrins rising ahead above the Eastern Dévoluy Escarpment. As with many limestone valleys the far end has collapsed leaving a bar, which is avoided by the path climbing to the right. This leads to a fine meadow, which lies beneath the towering Roche Courbe. On the south-eastern side of the meadow a track is followed that winds round below a shepherd's hut, the Cabane du Chorum Clot, before making its way down a broad ridge. Here GR93 shortcuts the track, and heads more or less due east. Some way after crossing a white limestone-chip track the GR starts to curve round to the north and then enters the hamlet of le Grand Villard. From there the D217 lane, still GR93, passes through two more hamlets, le Seresq and then Truchières, before cutting down through the fields towards St Disdier. This village lies at the head of the gorge leading out of the Dévoluy to the north. The gorge penetrates the high limestone cliffs that encircle this exquisite green valley. High above the far side of St Disdier stands the XIth century Mère Eglise; its spire is already visible from near the Cabane du Chorum Clot.

Just above St Disdier the GR rejoins the D217 and the route continues on this lane to a cross roads. The comfortable Hotel la Neyrette www.la-neyrette.com/hotel/ lies a short distance south of the village down the lane on the far side of this junction. The hotel in 2017 seems to be considerably more expensive in real terms than it was 2008, although it is doubtless still a pleasant stopover. As a less costly alternative, there is a gîte d'étape in the village of St Disdier http://www.gite-devoluy.com/. This lies beside GR93 and from their website this gîte d'étape looks like a good option.

The cliffs of the eastern escarpment of the Dévoluy, seen from la Neyrette at sunset

Day 5: St Disdier to St-Bonnet-en-Champsaur (1,023m)
28.4 km, up 1,655m, down 1,697m, high point the Col la Saume 1,704m, 9h22

This is a long walk, which in places requires careful attention to navigation. Much of the route continues on GR93. Starting from the far side of the road outside the hotel, a path leads north-northwest to the village of St Disdier, where GR93 is rejoined. This path then climbs eastwards to the Mère Eglise before bypassing loops in the road that winds uphill from the church. After passing through the hamlets of les Bas and Haute Gicons the GR contours on a rough road at the base of the Montagne de St-Gicon. Where the road forks, the GR heads right downhill and then crosses a bridge over a torrent. The rough road then climbs past the farm at la Chastre and continues southwards to le Collet. Some 1.3km along the road heading south from this village GR93 follows a footpath that goes up to the left into the Combe la Mayt. It then climbs to a ridge on the right of the combe and continues on this to a track, where there are fine views back across the valley to the peaks of the western Dévoluy escarpment, crossed on the previous day (photograph page 2). The track continues south-eastwards to the D17 road, which is followed eastwards to a hairpin bend. Here the GR continues straight ahead across the open pasture, climbing gently to the Col la Saume. Looking east from the col the escarpment falls steeply to the River Drac, beyond which rise the snow-capped peaks of the Écrins.

The path on the far side descends spectacularly, but safely, through a zigzag before heading south-eastwards across the steep escarpment. After passing through a cluster of scrubby trees the GR joins the narrow road from the Col de Noyer at a hairpin bend. This road provides a dramatic hill climb for cyclists and is sometimes included in the Tour de France. After going downhill on the road to the apex of the next loop, the GR leaves the road. It now follows a track that takes a southerly up and down course through the forest on the slopes of the eastern Dévoluy escarpment. Frequent side tracks and infrequent way-marks make it important to pay attention to route finding. After 5km the path reaches a clearing and the tiny Cabane des Pierres (below). Here our route turns left and climbs eastwards on a grassy track to the Pres la Chaup, leaving the GR, which heads southwards up the scree to the Col de Chetive. Our grassy track peters out on the meadow, but continue walking above the tree line until, after 1.2km, the forest curls up across the meadow. Now follow a track that descends east-north-eastwards through the woods to a well-made route forestière. This is followed to the right, for 2.7 km as it winds its way round the hillside. Eventually, after going through a hairpin bend and turning to the west, the route follows a path to the left at the next bend. This descends to the village of les Atards, but there are a number of side tracks and no way-marks, so careful navigation is required. On reaching the road it is necessary to trudge south-eastwards down to the bridge over the Drac and onwards to St Bonnet. On the north side of the town the comfortable Logis Hotel la Cremaillère https://www.logishotels.com/en/hotel/hotel-la-cremaillere-1268 is set in spacious grounds and is a good place to recover after this long tiring walk.

The Cabane des Pierres with the massive scree slopes beneath the Col de Chetive behind

Day 6: St-Bonnet-en-Champsaur to Chaillol (1,455m)
21.8km, up 1,735m, down 1,307m, high point the Barry 2,271m, 7h57

The somewhat tortuous route out of St Bonnet through the hamlets of les Aliberts and les Payas to the Col de la Blache and the junction with GR50 is a

From Vercors to the Queyras Alps

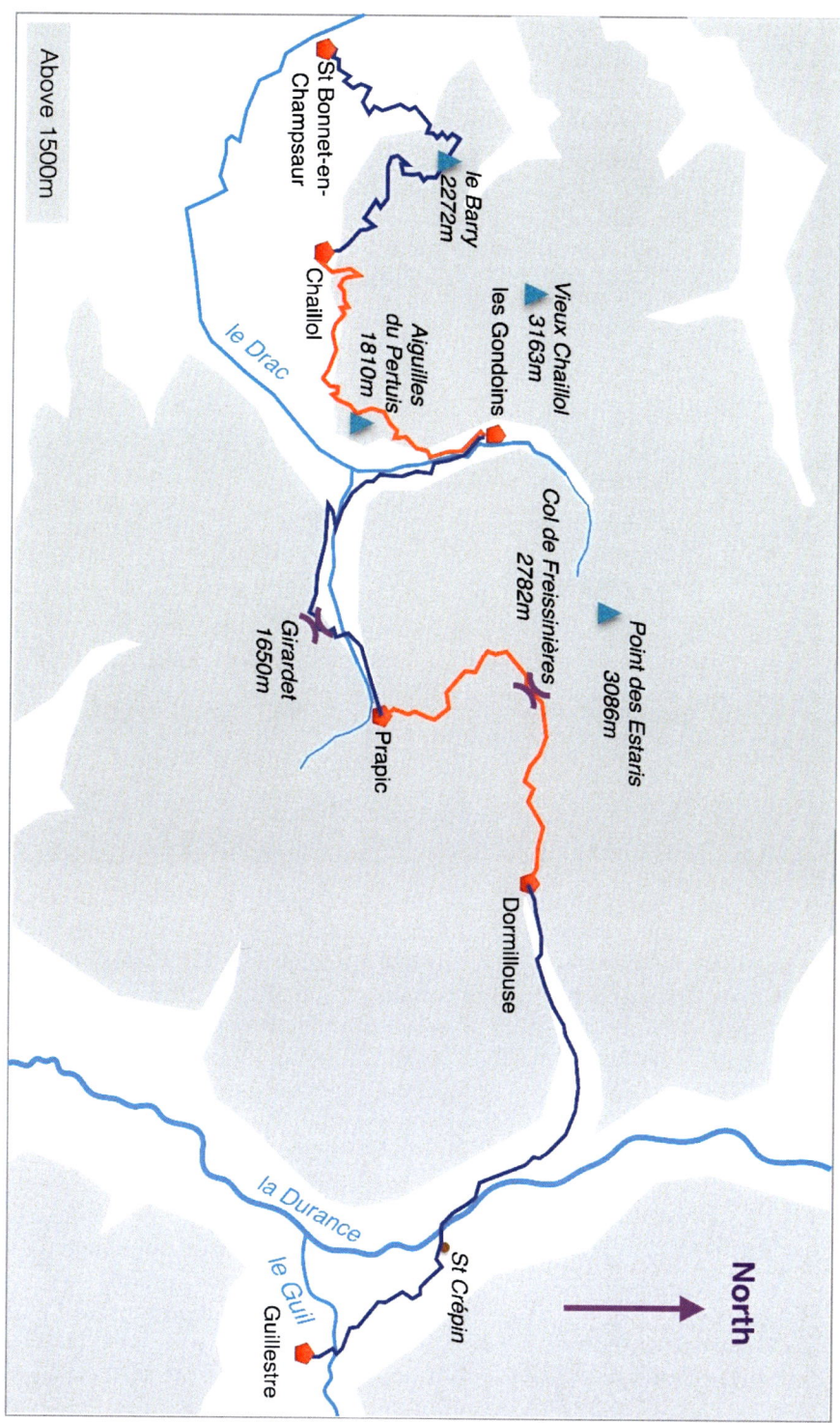

Days 6 to 10 St Bonnet-en-Champsaur through the Écrins to Guillestre

delight, especially when early morning sunlight is still casting long shadows. This route follows tracks and short stretches of country lane and there are great views back to the wooded hills walked over the previous afternoon. From the Col de la Blache it is a short descent north-eastwards on GR50 to the hamlet of les Infournas Hauts. Here the real climb starts as the route follows the GR that winds up a steep zigzagging grassy track through widely-spaced larches that are interspersed with wild rose bushes. The path levels off as it reaches a clearing with a large maison forestière to the left at the far side.

The steep final ascent to the Col de Cendrie and the start of the ridge of the Barry

While GR50 continues on a rough road eastwards from the clearing our route follows a forest track to the left that heads up the steep hillside through conifer woods. At 1782m the track becomes a path, which leaves the woods for strenuously-steep hillside (seen above, with the sharp hills of the Eastern Dévoluy in the background). Here the path climbs in zigzags, through a natural rock garden, to the Col de Cendrie. Alpenrose cover the greener slopes on the northern side of the col and the conical summit of Vieux Chaillol dominates the head of the valley in the east. The way forward is along a sharp ridge running southeast to a high point, le Barry. Red dots on the map justifiably indicate this is a delicate route to the Col de l'Escalier. In places the airy way along the crête is a scramble and there is some exposure. The IGN Map shows it is possible to avoid the ridge by descending north from Col de Cendrie and picking up a path well below the ridge that traverses to another path leading up to the Col de l'Escallier. Alternatively it is possible to stick to GR50 and avoid le Barry altogether, but this would be to miss a fine, if delicate, high mountain route.

From Col de l'Escalier a well graded path contours round the hillside to the south making one long zigzag before rejoining GR50 and continuing on this to Chaillol 1,600. To get to the Auberge l'Ocanière www.auberge-ocaniere.fr in the old village of Chaillol it is necessary to leave GR50 and walk down through the Chaillol 1,600 ski resort. This simple hotel is a good stopover for walkers. As an alternative there is an excellent gîte d'étape in the next village, les Marrons, described for Day 1 Chapter 7.

Day 7: Chaillol to Les Gondoins (1,311m)
18.3 km, up 1,418m, down 1,532m, high point above Aiguilles du Pertuis 1,850m, 6h52

If it is a fine day the outstanding walk over southern ridge of the Vieux Chaillol that is described for Day 2 in Chapter 7 should be considered. Nevertheless, the walk set out here, which is suitable for overcast days, is very enjoyable in its own right. This walk follows GR50, which skirts high above the valleys of the Drac and its tributary the Drac Blanc. Note the IGN map spells Gondoins as Gondouins. The former spelling, used by the locals, is used here.

The bergerie by the Riou Mort

After walking through the adjacent village of les Marrons a lane that becomes a track is followed along the western bank of the dry Riou Mort, to GR50. Half way up the Riou is a bergerie (above). In late June the eastbound GR50 is lined with a mass of white St Bruno's lilies and drifts of blue geraniums. When the path reaches point 1603m on the map the way forward on GR50 has been closed since 2015 because of repeated rock falls. The deviation heads south-eastwards on a footpath that passes through the hamlet of les Poranches before rejoining the original GR50. This then descends to a low point above the village of les Bonnets. Here, just below the path an underground river emerges, with the water tumbling noisily down the hillside. The path then traverses across steep granite boulder fields to a forest track that passes round another valley before emerging onto open hillside just below the hamlet of les Richards. This little settlement stands proud on the flat narrow top of a promontory that overlooks the confluence of the Drac Blanc with the Drac Noir. The former flows past Les Gondoins from the north, while the Drac Noir comes from the east. The road from the hamlet winds down the hill to the right, but our route continues straight ahead on GR50 as a path that climbs up steep hillside. After a zigzag section through sparse woodland the path continues across flowered alp until, some 200m vertically above the village, it joins a track for a short distance. Soon the GR leaves this track and climbs through woods above the Drac Blanc, passing a dugout pine water trough, before reaching the high point of the day. Here the path comes into the open and crosses seriously steep rocky hillside with a spectacular view past prominent pinnacles, les Aiguilles du Pertuis, to the river some 650m below. The path here is exposed but well-made and should not cause problems for those with a reasonable head for heights. The descent is in long zigzags to a junction of paths above the village of le Clappier. While the right branch, GR50, goes down to the village, our route continues to traverse for a while to a point where there is a fine view up the valley (photo end of Chapter 7). From there the path winds down to the Drac Blanc and then continues along its gravely north shore. It is necessary to wade through the icy stream that drains the valley headed by the Vieux Chaillol to reach the road that leads to the hamlet of les Gondoins and the Auberge/Gîte d'Étape des Gondoins, +33492559078 or +33698258597. This good stopover is a converted ancient farm house down by the river.

The bridge carrying the GR50 across the Drac Noir

Day 8 les Gondoins to Prapic (1,590m)
19.5 km, up 973m, down 725m, high point at Girardet 1,650 m, 5h55

The relatively gentle walk today heads south from les Gondoins on the D944a lane that runs along the east side of the Drac Blanc. GR 50 joins the lane at the pont des Eyrauds and a short distance after passing through the hamlet of les Eyrauds the route follows GR50 left onto a leafy track. This pleasant way leads to les Garnauds, where the GR crosses the main valley road diagonally to the left and then continues on a broad stony track parallel to the north bank of the Drac Noir. After crossing a side stream the GR comes to a substantial, long wooden footbridge over the main river (above). On the far side of this bridge there is a long climb westwards on a path that heads diagonally up the steep, wooded southern side of the valley. Just below the village of Serre-Eyrauds the path reaches a horizontal track that runs some 200m above the river. The route

From Vercors to the Queyras Alps

heads left, along this track, leaving GR50 and contouring eastwards through woods and fields. It is easy, but pleasant walking with glimpses of the village of Orcières on the opposite hillside, lying below the less appealing and sprawling ski station of Orcières-Merlette. The track ends at the village of les Audiberts and the route continues up the road through the village. After two hairpin bends a track to the left is followed that climbs north-eastwards. Soon a steep path is taken to the right that climbs to the highpoint of the day at Girardet. The path ends at a clearing, from where a track heads north-eastwards. Initially this passes below meadows. At the end of June these are packed with an exceptionally spectacular array of wild flowers (below). Now the track becomes wider and enters forest, zigzagging gently down to the buildings marked as Chalet on the IGN map[3]. The track then becomes a steep concrete drive that joins a lane, which is followed to the right across a ford. At the junction with another lane a right turn leads past the drive to les Chabauds and winds down to a bridge over the Drac Noir, where it continues to the village of les Fourés. Here the route turns right onto the now-quiet valley road, which is followed eastwards to its end just before the beautiful and car-free village of Prapic. This village has stone-paved streets and a fascinating collection of ancient houses. Gîte/Auberge Jabiore (+33 4 92 55 75 10), in the central square of the village, provides a good stopover. Prior booking is required outside the summer season.

Early summer flowers in the fields near Giardet

Day 9 – Prapic to Dormillouse (1,681m)
17.9 km, up 1,334m, down 1,185m, high point Col des Freissinières 2,782 m, 6h27

The route follows a track northwards from Prapic that makes its way along a tributary of the Drac Noir, the torrent de Blaisil. After crossing the torrent the track becomes a path that climbs up the ever steepening valley, appropriately termed les Pisses. Where the path divides at 1,850m, the route deviates from the standard path, marked in magenta on the map and the left fork is followed. This is shown by black dashes on the map. It is a good shortcut that heads up

---

[3] The forest track between Girardet to the Chalet is relatively new. The map shows a path shortcutting zigzags in this track, which was followed in 2008, but in September 2016 this was found to be rather overgrown through lack of use and might be best avoided.

beside a cascading stream called the Torrent du Lac du Col. At the top of the falls the path crosses the stream, but our route stays on the right bank of the stream, which flows through a pleasant alpine meadow. On reaching the télésège du Gnourou, this ski-lift is followed uphill to join the standard path. The line of this shortcut along the Torrent du Lac du Col more-or-less coincides with a ski touring route shown on the IGN map. Also this alternative route avoids a delicate section on the standard path after the Lac des Pisses that passes beneath the Roche Rousse. After rejoining the standard path the route heads westwards past several small tarns and then turns north to the shores of the Grand Lac des Esteris. The route on from the big lake climbs up a path across slatey gravel to the Col de Freissinières at 2,782m. The view west (below) looks down from the col to the blue Grand Lac

The view west from the Col de Freissinières with the Vieux Chaillol in the background

The mountain scenery of the upper Freissinières valley is impressive, with the peaks on either side rising to over 3,000m. The climb down from the col is on a good zigzagging path. After 450m descent the valley changes direction and the double white peak of Monte Viso comes into sight. This lies beyond the hills on the right of the valley and is some 55 km away to the east as the crow flies. At 3,841m Monte Viso stands well above all its neighbours and apparently can be seen from the summit of each of the peaks over 4,000m in the European Alps. This is highlighted in the title of Will McElwin's book 'In Monte Viso's Horizon'. His account of a very individual approach to climbing all of the 4000m peaks in the European Alps is a classic and a great read.

From the bend in the valley the broken rock and snow progressively give way to grass and finally lush flower-filled meadows. Roads and motorable tracks end at the foot of the rock band that crosses the valley to the east of Dormillouse. Consequently the scenery is marvelously unaffected by human endeavour; indeed in places the grass and flowers have reclaimed the path. In early summer alpenrose are abundant and the small pyramids of pink vanilla orchids are a striking feature in the grassland. The granite boulder-field immediately below the bend swallows up the stream flowing from the upper valley. This reappears some way further down as an impressive resurgence. Nearer Dormillouse, waterfalls cascading precipitously from the almost vertical valley walls become regular features. When the village eventually comes into view, it is still nearly an hour's walk to the gîte.

Dormillouse is inhabited all the year round. It is an ancient settlement that was a stronghold and refuge for Protestants in earlier centuries. The inhabitants were persecuted, particularly in the 14th and 15th centuries, by the Catholic establishment, spearheaded by the zealous Bishop of Embrun. Access to the village from the lower Freissinières valley is only by foot. A path to Dormillouse from the upper valley enters by the higher north part of the village. The Gîte d'Ecole http://www.dormillouse.fr/le-gite-de-lecole lies some way below this path, next to the church. It is open throughout the year and understandably is popular both with walkers and ski tourers.

Waterfall on the path down to Viollins from Dormillouse

Day 10 – Dormillouse to Guillestre (1,007m)
26.0 km, up 749m, 1,446m down, high point at the start 1,681m, 7h14

A path heads east from the gîte traversing across the steep northern wall of the valley. After a while this passes beneath a waterfall (above) and then zigzags down to a shaded lane that runs along the valley floor. This is followed eastwards to the pretty village of Viollins. Some 0.3km past the village a right turn from the road, leads to a bridge across the foaming river (below) and then a track is followed eastwards that runs through pleasant woodland on the south bank. While walking along this track there are glimpses, through the trees of the village of Freissinières, which lies on the hillside on the far side of the River Biasse. Five km below Viollins, just before Pallon the two sides of the Freissinières valley come close together and the river flows into a small lake behind a barrage. At Pallon the route joins 3 grande randonnées, GR50, GR541 and GR653D. The last of these runs from the Italian border at Montgenèvre to Arles, where it joins the pilgrimage route to Santiago de Compostela. Our route follows the GR653D for most of the second half of this day.

The 'boiling' River Biasse in the Freissinières valley below Viollins

From Pallon this GR continues west-southwestwards on the D38 road, as it traverses high on the west side of the Durance Valley. After the village of le Cambon the D38 turns to the left starting its long zigzagging descent to the Durance valley floor, but GR653D, goes straight ahead on the D38a through the village of Champcella. Some way beyond the village the GR turns left from the road and continues as a path down to the D38. The GR then follows the general line of this road down to Chanteloube, while shortcutting most of its zigzags. On the far side of Chanteloube and just before reaching the metal bridge over the Durance there is a glider field to the right. After crossing the bridge and the main valley road the route continues into the south end of St Crépin. There is much new development here, but the recent buildings fit in well with those in the old walled town. St Crépin is a convenient lunch stop.

The walk on to Guillestre continues following GR653D on tracks and country lanes through the villages on the eastern hillside above the Durance. From the southeast end of the village of Eygliers the hillside drops to the river Guil, which drains the Queyras Hills. Here the Guil has cut a deep gorge through the rock. Guillestre stands on a plateau that extends from the top of the cliff on the opposite side of the river, while the citadel of Mont-Dauphin is southwest of Eygliers on the northern lip of the gorge. This citadel overlooks the confluence of the Guil and Durance. A dusty track, with large unstable gravel, contours down east-south-eastwards from Eygliers to the Pont du Samoust over the Guil. On the far side a steep, thankfully-shaded path, marked with black dashes on the 2017 IGN map, zigzags up the cliff to a grassy plateau. Guillestre lies some 0.6km across this plateau, which is irrigated generously with small channels between the fields. The Logis Hotel — Catinat Fleuri http://www.catinat-fleuri.com provides a comfortable stopover in Guillestre.

Pics de la Font Sancte reflected in Lac Miroir

Day 11 - Pied du Mélezet (1,702m) to Maljasset (1,910m)
12.1 km, up 1,135m, 943m down, high point the Col Girardin 2,695m, 4h48

On the basis of an ominous weather-forecast, the author decided to reduce the length of the route originally planned to get to Maljasset by taking a taxi to Ceillac. This relatively short ride cuts both distance and ascent from the original challenging walk that would have passed the Refuge de Basse Rua and then crossed the Col des Houerts (2,871m). The route described here is an enjoyable way south on GR5. This walk has recently become one day in the three-day GR de Pays du Tour de la Font Sancte. The second day reverses the high-level part of the walk originally planned for this day. While the third day from the Refuge de Basse Rua to Ceillac is described for Day 13 in Chapter 6.

Starting a little west of Ceillac at the Pied du Mélezet the modified route follows GR 5 up a steep, well made, path winding through rocks to the picturesque Lac Miroir, which lives up to its name (above). From this lake the

Mountains of the Provençal Rim

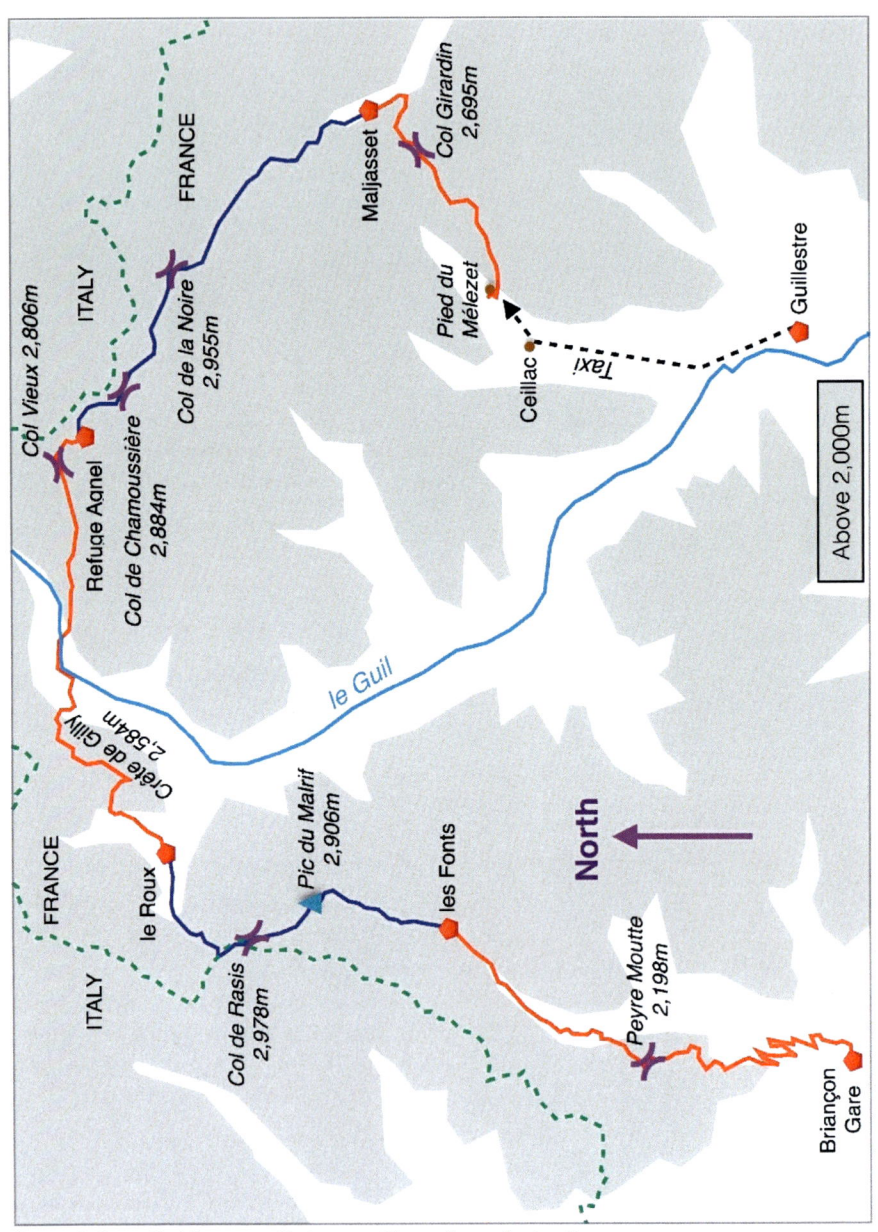

Last 5 days Guillestre to Briançon Gare through the Queyras

route continues to the Lac Ste Anne. Here the ground is more barren, the blue-green of the lake contrasting with the rock and scree of the surrounding hills. The Chapel of Ste Anne stands above the eastern shore of the lake.

The walk to the Col Girardin becomes progressively steeper. In the last section it zigzags up fine, flaky, compressed yellow gravel, dotted with defiant gentians and other delicate alpine flowers. From the summit, there are great views back down the valley (below). Onwards to the south the sharp peaks of the Chambeyron hills rise on the far side of the deep upper valley of the Ubaye. A walk through these hills is described in Chapter 7.

Looking north from the Col de Girardin to the Lac Ste Anne

There are alternative routes for the descent to the Ubaye Valley, but GR5 heads down from the Col Girardin towards the village of la Barge. Although steep, this descent through flower-filled meadows is a delight and perfectly safe. From the junction of the path with the D25 lane northeast of la Barge it is about a km up the tarmac to the car-free village of Maljasset. Among the jumble of old houses and narrow lanes in the village there are two gîtes. Also, in a house that rents rooms, there is a useful épicerie in the basement. Outside its door a rope leads to a bell two stories above that serves to alert the shopkeeper that a customer has arrived

The excellent Gîte/Auberge de la Cure, http://maljassetgite.fr/ is a picturesque old house on the side facing the river. Don't be put off by its upper side where the door may be barred. Majasset is worth a visit, not least for the wonderful walks involved in getting there and moving on.

Maljasset to the Refuge Agnel (2,580m)
18.6km, up 1,578m, 917 m down, high point Col de la Noire 2,955m, 6h50

The ascent of the upper valley of the Ubaye is long and varied. From 1.2km east of Maljasset this beautiful valley lacks a road of any sort, keeping it free from intensive agriculture and most visitors. After the first hour's walk from Maljasset the Ubaye splits delta-wise into multiple streams, as it crosses a broad stony flood-plane. The branches of the river are bordered by willow thicket. Beyond this flood-plain the valley divides. Leading to the northeast is a gorge, where our route climbs on a path that traverses high above the river, crossing unstable, grey, gritty gravel. After a while the gorge opens out into broad meadows where there is an easy 4km walk before the valley winds round to the east and the shallow col comes into view. This col marks the border with Italy.

The Col Noire with the Tête de Toillies in the background

After passing to the left of the Cabane du Col and well before the border there is a red arrow on a rock to the left of the path indicating the direction of the Col de la Noir. This route climbs alongside the stream, the Béal du Jas du Col. It is marked as a ski trail rather than a footpath on the map; indeed there is no discernible path. Nevertheless, a way at first marked by small cairns and then by yellow painted arrows, follows the stream up the gully. At the top of the gully the route joins a path heading west-northwest. This is followed, ignoring paths leading off to the west. After 0.25km a path is taken that turns to the north and then northeast. This climbs up a broad grassy spur that leads to a hanging valley with the Lac de la Noire at its base. The path passes to the left of the lake and climbs steadily to the Col de la Noire (above). Far from being black much of rock at the col and on the descent has an attractive cupric green hue that contrasts with the local orange granite. The rock spike of the Tête de Toillies dominates the view along the ridge to the east, while 450m below on the north side of the col lies the Refuge de la Blanche.

The route descends to the refuge from where a path is followed that climbs north-eastwards. After a km the marked path heads east, but our route continues without difficulty climbing north-northeast across trackless hillside until it joins the GR58: Tour du Queyras and turns right on this heading for the Col de Chamoussière. From this col the snow-capped peak of Monte Viso, which had been seen first from the Freissinières valley four days before, comes into close view. A black slate-chip path winds down between the rocks towards the Refuge Agnel. On approaching the refuge Monte Viso slips below the horizon and the cone of the Pain de Sucre (3,208m) comes to dominate the view ahead (below).

The Pain de Sucre in the evening sun

The refuge is large and relatively modern http://www.refugeagnel.com/. It lies just off the mountain road that passes over the Col Agnel into Italy. Consequently, many of the clientele arrive by car. At 2,580m, this refuge is the highest stopover of the trip, but after the peace and tranquility of the Upper Ubaye the crowds in this refuge may come as a rude shock. The owners run an efficient service and provide ample food.

Day 13: Refuge Agnel to Le Roux (1,735m)
21.9 km, up 1,428m, down 2,269m, high point col Vieux 2,806m, 8h00

This day starts with a climb eastwards, still on GR58, out of the shadow of the high hills to the Col Vieux where the trade-route up the northwest flank of the Pain de Sucre starts. This looks steep and interesting, but the climb would add considerably to an already long day. Northwards down the Val Bouchouse lies Lac Foréant, which, in the early morning, falls in the shadow of the massive slab of the Crête de la Taillante. From the lip of this first hanging valley there is a fine view down a verdant second valley, which also has a lake in its base, the Lac Égorgéou (below). This second lake is emerald green, reflecting a bottom of granite sand.

The view down the Val Bouchouse to the Lac Égorgéou

The descent from Lac Égorgéou passes waterfalls and spreads of alpenrose. The previously-screened Monte Viso comes into full view with its towering twin peaks. Then the path enters pine woods on the final descent to the west bank of the infant river Guil. The route goes over the shingles on the left side of the river, past the first bridge and crossing a second bridge into the hamlet of la Monta. The local gîte d'étape http://www.refuge-queyras-la-monta.com/ is a good lunch stop.

From la Monta there is a long, but pleasant climb of 961m on GR58 through fields, pine woods and then alpine meadows to the Crête de Gilly. The walking traffic of the lower Bouchouse valley is not evident here and the path westwards along the crête (below) is a delight. The path still, GR58, leaves the crête at the Collette de Gilly, descending on the eastern side through groves of alpenrose and then conifer forest. After descending north-north-eastwards to a forestry track this is followed westwards at about 2,000m for some 1.1km. Then the GR58 splits and our route continues on the GR58 variant to the right. This descends west-north-westwards to a bridge over a stream and follows the variant GR into the pleasant village of le Roux. Here the stopover is in the welcoming, comfortable Gîte d'Étape Le Cassu http://www.gite-lecassu.com/.

Striding along the Crête de Gilly

Day 14: Le Roux to Les Fonts (2,040m)
14.8 km, 1,494m up, 1,201m down, high point 2,921m Col de Rasis, 6h06

Distance-wise this is the second shortest day of the walk, but there is a tough and exhilarating climb up to the frontier ridge and along this before descending to les Fonts. The start continues on the GR58 variant, which heads north from the gîte on the lane that runs to the east of the torrent de la Montette. After crossing the second bridge over this stream a path zigzags up the hill past some ruins to a chapel. Here the route continues to the left at a fork on GR58 variant, climbing relentlessly west-north-westwards for 876m to the col des Thures on the international border. The path onward follows the frontier ridge south-westwards before dipping to the Italian side of the border and crossing a boulder field. From there the path climbs again to the frontier at the Col de Rasis. On the far side of this col a descent into France on scree leads to a small lake and a long traverse follows below the Grand Glaiza. At first this is on grass, studded in early summer with vivid blue small gentians. Later steep scree is crossed as the path edges up to the Col de Malrif (below). Next follows a short climb south-westwards up a ridge to the Pic du Malrif (2,906m). The Écrins are much closer now in the northwest (photo page 6). To the south are the hills of Southern Queyras and Monte Viso (below).

The Southern Queyras Ridge and Monte Viso from the Col de Malrif

The north-westwards descent from the Pic de Malrif to Les Fonts on GR58 is a pleasant stroll through the alpine meadows that lie on either side of the torrent de Pierre Rouge. At this stage the mass of the Roc Rouge dominates the view behind and to the left. Les Fonts lies at the junction of two high valleys. The Refuge de Cervières http://www.montourduqueyras.fr/fr/il4-refuge_i38263-refuge-des-fonts.aspx is one of the cluster of ancient houses that make up the hamlet. This is an attractive old building and the owners run the refuge in a friendly, welcoming and efficient way.

Day 15: Les Fonts to Briançon (1,212m)
25.0 km, up 895m, 1,727m down, high point 2,204m Peyre Moutte, 7h26

For the last day the route crosses the river from the refuge and follows a track on the far side. After 2.7km it crosses back over the river to the valley road by a rickety bridge and soon moves to a track through meadows to the right of the road, passing three clusters of old houses. Many of these have been refurbished, but they all carry characteristic gutters formed from a scooped out half trunk of a thin fir tree. These are held in place by the bases of saplings pinned to the eaves, with one of the roots of each sapling forming a cradle for the gutter. From the grassy track Mont Pelvoux, the most prominent giant of the eastern Écrins, appears framed between the walls of the valley (below). Eventually the track returns to the road and this is followed as it climbs through an S bend. Then our route leaves the road on a track to the right, passing below the houses of the hamlet of la Chau. From there a path is followed west-north-westwards up a broad ridge on the left side of the Peyre Moutte. The strategic importance of this frontier valley and the ancient military presence in and around Briançon starts to become apparent, for below a stone defensive wall, the Mur des Aîttes spans the narrowest part of the valley.

Mont Pelvoux from the valley below les Fonts

At around 2,200m a path is followed to the left that traverses west-south-westwards round the hillside. For a while, it is a fine track made for military rather than agricultural purposes. It passes through a barrier of rusty coils of barbed wire, which conveniently have been cut to allow access. With precision the track follows a slight but steady downward angle as it contours the hillside. Where the hillside curves towards the northwest there is a magnificent view of the Eastern Écrins, reaching high above a stand of conifers.

After some time the hillside becomes steeper and in places the track has fallen away leaving only an unstable and exposed path. At one point there was a pole of dubious security (below) that had been placed to bridge a steep gully where the track had slipped into the abyss. Soon after this obstacle the route joins a metaled lane, which makes long zigzags down the mountain linking a series of abandoned forts. After a while, a notice designed for uphill traffic indicates the area is military ground and that civilians should keep out. The order was from the 1930's and the notice is almost as old, so presumably this can be ignored. It is reassuring for walkers that the map only indicates "circulation automobile interdite". Eventually the road reaches the valley floor just above the dam of a lake. Below the barrage a dusty boulder-strewn track leads to the outskirts of Briançon and the floor of the main Durance valley, where it joins GR5 for the final km into town. The Hotel de la Chaussée www.hotel-de-la-chaussee.com is one of a number of hotels that provides convenient accommodation and board near the station.

A dubious substitute for the eroded path on the way to Briançon

Return from Briançon

Trains from Briançon run to Aix en Provence and Marseille in the south. The train to Gap continues to Die, Vallance and Lyon and there are trains from Gap to Grenoble. There are also bus services between Briançon and Grenoble.

3 CHAPTER
GORGES AND WATERSHEDS OF THE CÉVENNES
A 12 day walk of 248.7km, with 12,596m ascent

from Cazilhac to la Bastide-Puylaurent

The Southern Cévennes region is a limestone country with deep river gorges splitting plateau land and intervening ridges. The rivers are tributaries of the Hérault, which flows southwards to the Mediterranean, giving its name to a wine-growing department of the Occitanie region.

Starting from Cazilhac, near Ganges the route described in this chapter heads south-westwards, for two days along the ridge of the Sérrane. It then descends into the steep-sided gorge of the River Vis, where a night is spent in the hamlet at the base of the Cirque de Navacelles. The following day the Vis is followed upstream to its dramatic resurgence from the limestone at les Moulins de la Foux. The walk then turns towards the northeast climbing out of the gorge and crossing a tranquil and richly floral plateau, before descending to le Vigan in the valley of l'Arre and leaving the Southern Cévennes.

From le Vigan the route follows a broad ridge northwards to the Pic de Barette and then descends its sharp eastern crête to the ancient village of Valleraugue on the banks of the upper reaches of the Hérault. The next day, Mont Aigoual, the second highest mountain in the Cévennes, is climbed by its southeast ridge. Its summit lies on the Atlantic-Mediterranean watershed and this dividing line is followed during the descent of the east ridge and throughout the next three days. The first of these days ends at the hill village of the Barre-des-Cévennes, while the second crosses the Col de Jalcrest to the tiny hamlet of Vieljouvès-Bas on the south side of the Montaigne du Bouges. After crossing the high point of this hill, the Signal de Ventalon, the route descends to the Croix de Berthel. Then it climbs to the headwaters of the Tarn, on the southeastern aspect of Mont Lozère, the highest hill in the Cévennes. From the east end of Mt Lozère the walk descends to Villefort and continues to the confluence of the rivers Altier, Chassezac and Borne at the Pied-de-Borne. The final stages climb over the granite hills of the Vivarais and Tenargue before heading west to la Bastide-Puylaurent, on the banks of the Allier, a major tributary of the Loire, where the walk ends.

In mid-May these exquisitely beautiful hills are often all but deserted during the week and in general the tracks and paths are one's own. This is the season when the flowers are at their best. There is an all-pervading scent of the golden broom that covers many of the hillsides. White and yellow narcissi as well as wild tulips flourish on the high pastures and there is an abundance of wild orchids, particularly the yellow and crimson elderflower orchids. The first 4 days of this walk were done in the last days of April 2017, while the walk from le Vigan to la Bastide-Puylaurent was completed in mid-May 2013.

Yellow Elderflower Orchid

Summary of Cévennes walk

Day 1: Cazilhac (149m) to le Mas de Luzière St-André-de-Buèges (140m)
23.7km, up 1,045m, down 1,061m, high point Roc Blanc 911m, 7h03

Day 2: Le Mas de Luzière to Gîte d'Étape le Ranquas (574m)
16.8km, up 1,123m down 694m, high point summit Peyre Martine 782m, 5h36

Day 3: Gîte d'Étape le Ranquas to Navacelles (328m)
14.9km, up 903m, down 1,149m high point les Rajols 679mm 5h06

Day 4: Navacelles to le Vigan (233m)
27.1km, up 1,109m, down 1,205m, high point by Rocher du Marquis 672m, 7h55

Day 5: le Vigan (266m) to Valleraugue (370m)
17.2km, up 1,318m, down 1,182m, high point the Pic de Barette 1,318m, 6h17

Day 6: Valleraugue to Gîte-d'Étape d'Aire de Côte (1,085m)
13.9km, up 1,560m, down 847m, high point Mt Aigoual 1,565m, 5h50

Day 7: Aire de Côte to Barre-des-Cévennes (948m)
23.0km, up 652m, down 793m, high point 1,180m near start, 6h00

Day 8: Barre-des-Cévennes to Vieljouvès-Bas (932m)
24.3km, up 993m, down 1,010m, high point 1,100m Mont Mars, 6h50

Day 9: Vieljouvès-Bas to le Mas de la Barque (1,417m)
25.3km, up 1,148, down 669m, high point 1,437m near Senegriere on Mt Lozère, 7h20

Day 10: le Mas de la Barque to Pied-de-Borne (328m)
23.9km, up 619m, down 1,711m, high point 1,449m Pre de la Dame, 6h00

Day 11: Pied-de-Borne to Loubaresse (1,210m)
21.5km, up 1,369m, down 501m, high point 1,210m Loubaresse, 8h00

Day 12: Loubaresse to la Bastide-Puylaurent (1,016m)
17.1km, 757m ascent, 938m descent, high point 1,264m Coulet de Pécovol, 5h45

Total 248.7km, with 12,596m ascent, average 20.7km, 1,049m ascent

From Mt Aigoual's east ridge looking over the southeast ridge to the Pic de Barette

Getting to les Norrias in the North of Cazilhac (226m)

Montpellier is the nearest large town served by both an airport and mainline trains. An hourly bus service from the Airport to the centre of Montpellier, takes about 15 minutes www.herault-transport.fr/fiche_horaire/120-mars.pdf. From the Station Occitanie in Montpellier a bus runs about every 3 hours to Ganges and takes some 1h15. The last bus leaves Montpellier at around 18.15 www.herault-transport.fr/fiche_horaire/108.pdf. The bus stop in Ganges is a few minutes walk from the comfortable Logis Hotel les Norrias in Cazilhac on the other side of the River Herault https://www.les-norias.fr/.

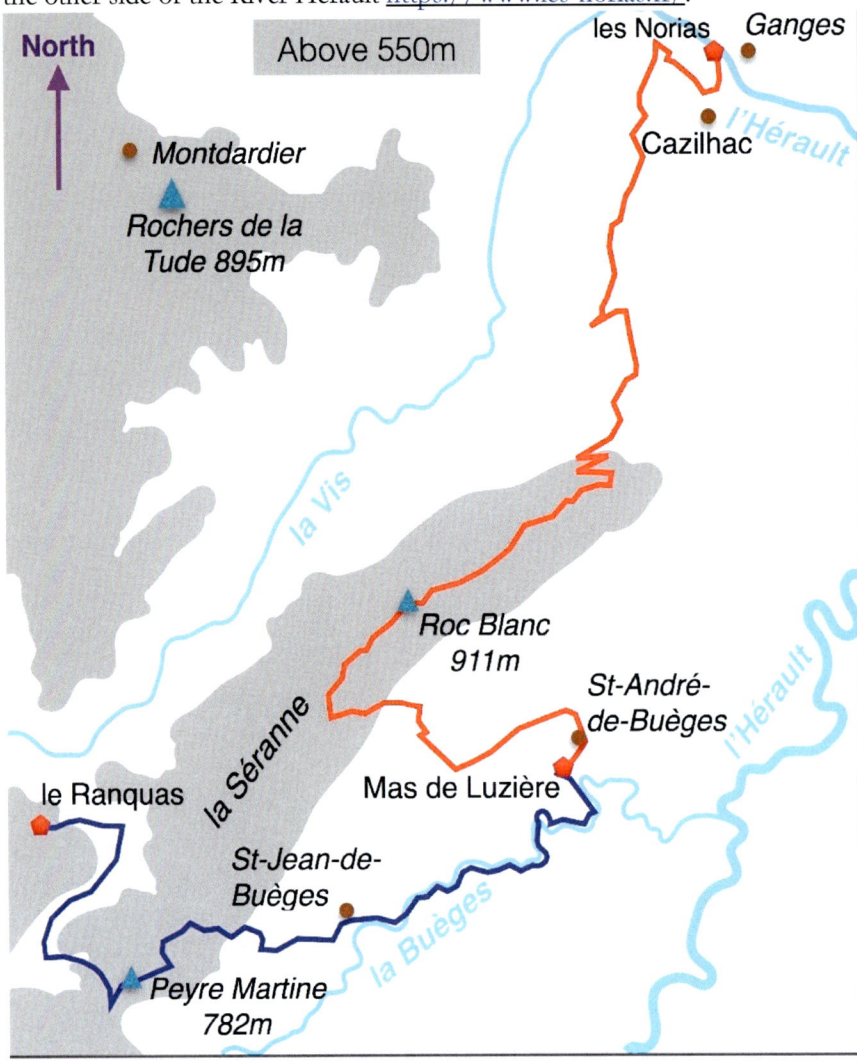

Cévennes walk Days 1 and 2

Day 1 Cazilhac to Mas de Luzière, St-André-de-Buèges (140m)
23.7km, up 1,045m, down 1,061m, high point Roc Blanc 911m, 7h03

The first day's walk climbs south-westwards on a broad, well-graded track up and along the lengthy ridge of the Séranne (below) to its west summit, the Roc Blanc. After the easy start there is an interesting, but straightforward scramble down the sharp limestone southwest ridge. After a while the ridge broadens and the path gradually makes its way round to the east, before making a steep descent to the lane that runs between St-Jean-de-Buèges and St-André-de-Buèges. The stopover for the night, the Logis hotel le Mas de Luzière lies a short distance southwest of St-André.

The Séranne Ridge seen in the left background from southwest of St Jean-de-Buèges

The start turns left out of the hotel and takes the first road on the right. A few metres up the road a narrow lane, with yellow way-marks, is followed to the left. This climbs steeply, winding round to the northwest, where it joins a broad stony track that continues the ascent, north-westwards, still with yellow way-marks. At 320m the gradient eases and the track goes through a hairpin bend at the Puech Pointu. It then gradually climbs west-south-westwards, reaching 478m after some 2km. On either side of the track there is dense squat forest. The track now descends gently and after one hairpin to the left reaches a crossing of tracks at 372m. The route and yellow way-marks follow the track that runs straight ahead to the south. At first this gains little height, as it gently undulates to the right of a broad ridge, gradually working its way round to the southwest. At 530m the track starts to go through 4 long zigzags, before reaching a telecommunications pylon at 681m. Now the track, still marked with occasional yellow flashes, heads to the the southwest, running a short way below the broad crest of the ridge of the Séranne. The hillside falls steeply to the left and the right border of the track is still covered with scrubby woodland. A signpost, located just after the pylon, indicates it is 3.5km to the summit. The track continues at a gradual incline below the crest of the ridge and finally climbs through 2 hairpin bends to the summit of the Séranne at 942m. In fine weather this is a major site for launching hang-gliders and paragliding.

Our route bypasses the main summit and continues southwest from the first of the hairpin bends on a narrower track that leads to the west summit, le Roc Blanc (911m). This rock has a large flat top with sides that drop precipitously to the north, south and west. It is a fine viewpoint in good weather. The the way onto the southwest ridge starts to the left of the track just as it reaches the rock. This is well way-marked with both yellow and blue paint marks. It is a bit of a scramble on the limestone ridge for some time, but this is not technically difficult if one sticks to the marked route. At around 800m the ridge becomes rounded and the way-marks show the route splits. The route to the left is followed. This continues as a narrow path that twists and turns passing bushes, small trees and crossing grassy clearings. At first the path heads southwestwards, then it turns to the west and flattens out for a while before it winds round to the south and descends to a flat, grassy clearing at 712m. Ignore the blue way-marks heading westwards (right) on a path past a large limestone menhir (standing stone). This path is labelled le Chemin de la Coupette on the map. Our route heads eastwards on this chemin. At first the way is not clear and a blue cross confusingly suggests this route is incorrect. Despite this, after going eastwards for a while a distinct path develops, which is labelled with both yellow and blue way-marks. This path steepens, starts zigzagging and becomes limestone scree underfoot. Where the path divides the yellow way-marked path is followed to the southwest passing through scrubby woodland. After a while this path descends more steeply to the south, eventually reaching flat open ground. There a track is followed that leads through fields to the D1 road at the 204m mark shown on the IGN 1:25k map. This road is followed to the left for 1.5km, before a right turn is made into the small village of St-André-de-Buèges. Hotel le Mas de Luzière http://luziere.fr lies some 0.65km beyond the village. This is an attractive and comfortable hotel, marked as l'Euzière on the IGN map. It has an excellent restaurant that specialises in serving well-selected, fine local wines.

The shaded river Buèges on the way to St-Jean-de-Buèges

Day 2, Mas de Luzière (140m) to le Ranquas (574m)
16.8km, up 1,123m down 694m, high point summit Peyre Martine 782m, 5h36

This delightful day starts with a riverside walk up the valley of the Buèges. This shy river flows below ground for some of its course, particularly in high summer. Where it runs along the surface the crystal-clear stream flows over shallow waterfalls beneath leafy trees (above). The walk passes through the picturesque ancient village of St-Jean-de-Buèges before climbing the steep escarpment to the right of the Cirque de la Séranne and then crossing the peak of the Peyre Martine, the highest point on the lip of the cirque. The route then descends across the plateau to the edge of the Gorges de la Vis before climbing to the Gîte d'Étape le Ranquas (labelled as Rancas on the IGN map).

From the Mas the route heads up the lane and just before the top of the rise turns left on a path through a wild meadow on the east side of a wood. In May this meadow is studded with Bee Orchids (below). At the far end of the meadow the path descends through the wood to a track by the side of the river.

Bee Orchid

43

The ford before St. Jeani-de-Buèges in gentle conditions

This track is followed westwards along the river bank, until, at the end of the wood it heads away from the river, circles a field and then returns to the Buèges. Here the route crosses an ancient stone humpback footbridge and follows the west and then southern bank of this beautiful shaded river. Some 3km further on the route crosses a ford. There are some rickety, unstable stepping stones, but the safer option is to cool and wash one's feet walking over the smooth concrete base of the ford (above). Should the Buèges be in spate (below) there is a route from the bridge along the north side of the river, which is also pleasant, but has less contact with the serenity of the stream. After the ford the route follows a lane that leads into a narrow street in the southwest corner of the ancient village of St Jean-de-Buèges. There are two bar-restaurants in St Jean if refreshment is required.

The walk continues on the western side of the village, to the left of the church. There, a lane way-marked with yellow flashes, is the start of the Circuit of le Peyre Martine. This climbs initially past cultivated fields before continuing on

The ford when the Buège was in spate at the end of April 2017

a shaded path, in a series of zigzags, up the steep escarpment. There are spectacular views as the path passes the Rocher du Caylaret (below). It then continues to a col with a grassy clearing. From there the path continues horizontally north-westwards passing a signpost indicating Circuit le Peyre Martine. Soon after this sign the route, still marked with yellow flashes, turns left (south-westwards) and climbs, through scrub, up a rounded hill, skirting to the right (north) of its summit. The path then continues to the summit of a second rounded hill, le Peyre Martine (782m). Here blue flashes mark a short detour to fine views of the Cirque de la Sérrane.

Rocher du Caylaret with St-Jean in the valley and the Pic St Loup in the distance

After returning to the yellow-flashed path this descends westwards across a complex series of limestone ribs to a col at 661m. Here a prominent signpost marks the way westwards towards the Chemin de St Guilhem-le-Desert (GR74). Our route is not-signposted and heads north-northeast from the col on the GR de Pays: Tour du Larzac Méridional. This path is marked with occasional red and white GR waymarks. It gradually winds round to the west as it descends through scrubby forest to a farm in the relatively flat Combe des Natges. On reaching a crossing of tracks the GR turns right following the track on the east side of the valley floor. After a while the track crosses the valley and continues on the far side. Later, the GR moves onto a path that forks to the left from the track, heading north-westwards and undulating through pleasant deciduous woodland. Finally the path makes a T junction with a larger path. Here the GR turns just north of west and climbs, at times in zigzags, to the Gîte d'Étape du Ranquas http://le.ranquas.free.fr. This delightful gîte d'étape, run by Nicole Vienney, is a good stopover and excellent value. The cubbyhole access to the dortoire where the author and his colleagues slept is quite interesting (below).

The interesting entrance to the dortoire at the Gîte d'Étape du Ranquas

Day 3 Gîte d'Étape du Ranquas to Navacelles (328m)
14.9km, up 903m, down 1,148m high point les Rajols 679mm 5h06

This relatively short, but delectable walk should not be rushed. At first the route follows the left lip of the Gorges de la Vis, before entering the village of St-Maurice-Navacelles. From there it turns northwards towards the edge of the gorge and then ziggzags down on the steep east flank of a spur to the southwestern bank of the River Vis. The walk then contours on an at-times-

Gorges and Watersheds of the Cévennes

exciting path on the west side of the gorge until it reaches the hamlet of Navacelles at the base of the Cirque des Navacelles.

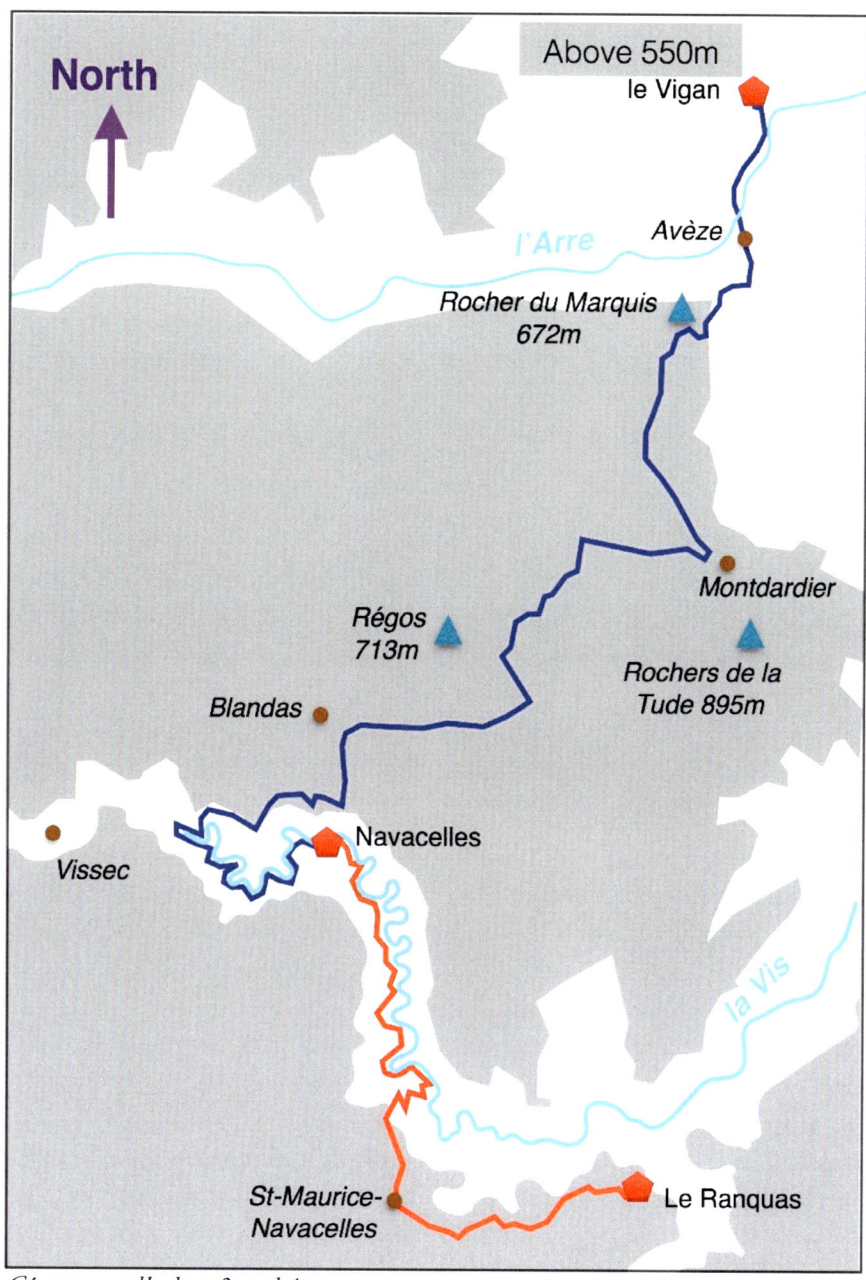

Cévennes walk days 3 and 4

The route heads west on the GR de Pays: Tour du Larzac Méridional. At first this follows the metaled lane from the gîte. It then descends to the right of the lane to a balcony path that contours along the southern lip of the Gorges de Vis. This is partially meadowland and in places goes through sparse woodland. There are fine views down to the base of the gorge and, in the east, back to the summit of the Séranne and the profile of its southwest ridge, descended on the first day. Eventually the GR leaves the lip of the gorge and continues west to the village of St-Maurice-Navacelles. Here GR7 is joined and followed north out of the village through meadowland. The grassland of this part of the plateau is filled with droves of the tall stemmed Asphodelus Albus, which are in bloom in April and May.

GR7 running above the aquaduct on the precipitous south wall of the Gorges de Vis

On reaching the lip of the gorge the GR zigzags down the steep eastern side of a spur projecting from the southern lip. The path is well-made, but might prove uncomfortable for someone nervous of heights. There is certainly no temptation to consider shortcutting the zigzags. Eventually the path reaches a track at the bottom of the gorge. The track is followed upstream, passing the impressive, but abandoned Mas du Pont. This grand house must have been accessed from downstream for there is hardly space for a path, let alone a track further up-river. After the next twist in the river the track starts to climb gradually to an EDF aqueduct. This historic and impressive canal was built between 1902 and 1907 and runs, from just upstream of Navacelles, for 12km to some 100m above Madières. The water then plunges to a hydroelectric plant on the riverside. The canal is an engineering tour de force. In places it flows along the cliffs (above) and sometimes goes through tunnels in the limestone. GR7 follows the track on the lower side of the aqueduct for some 1.5km. Then, where the canal disappears into the hillside, it climbs as a path in zigzags above the canal. After a while it starts to contour well above the canal, following an exciting course across the steep hillside and cliffs on the west side of the gorge. Eventually the path reaches a ridge above Navacelles and then descends to this picturesque hamlet, set in the Cirque des Navacelles. The hamlet consists of two clusters of houses. The lodging for the night is in the western cluster, halfway up the pedestrian street on the right. The Chambre/Table d'Hôte Ammonite of the Mas Guillou offers a warm welcome, comfortable and delightfully furnished rooms, together with excellent food http://masguilhou.wixsite.com/home/copie-de-l-ammonite. The same owners also run a cafe and a gîte d'étape a few meters down the street.

The resurgence of the Vis at the Moulins de la Foux

Day 4: Navacelles to the Hotel du Commerce le Vigan (233m)
27.1km, up 1,109m, down 1,205m, high point by Rocher du Marquis 672m, 7h55

This is a long varied day, with more delights in the Gorges de la Vis, especially the dramatic resurgence of the river from the limestone at the Moulins de la Foux (above). There is a fine walk out of the gorge followed by a delightful crossing of the flower-filled undulating plateau north of les Gorges de la Vis to Montdardier. The final section of the day follows GR 7 northwards off the plateau to the small town of le Vigan.

The lane at the top of the alley where the Ammonite lies is followed to the right. This leads to a hairpin bend in the road that winds down the south side of the gorge. After crossing this road the route follows a track, labelled with red and yellow way-marks, towards les Moulins de la Foux. As far as the resurgence the route is along the GR du Payes: Tour du Larzac Méridional. The track descends gradually, passing above the start of the aqueduct. It then levels off and continues as a path that traverses well above the river, before descending to the riverside, with the aid of fixed ropes. The ropes assist when the path is wet, but this section is neither difficult nor dangerous for a healthy walker. The path continues following the tortuous course of the river and eventually passes to the left of the buildings at les Poujols. Some 0.8km after this the path spits and the right fork leads down to the resurgence and the ancient mill buildings, les Moulins de la Foux. There are records of a mill at this site since the eleventh century and it has been rebuilt on several occasions. The existing ruins were secured and converted into a museum in 2000.

The Gorges de Vis from the Northern Rim above Navacells

The path from the mill crosses a stone bridge and then makes its way over rocks above the boiling river. From the far side there is a clear view of the flow of the river from the limestone. After the resurgence the path at first climbs south-eastwards, gradually making its way through forest with several fine tall cedars. On reaching the road that winds up the north side of the gorge, this is followed uphill for 0.8km. Then the second path is taken to the left that circles up the top part of the gorge, where there are fine views down the Vally of the Vis (above).

Shortley after reaching the lip of the gorge the path comes to an iron signpost. Here our route turns right (eastwards) across rough grass between shrubs. After about 0.2km a rocky viewpoint is reached at the rim of the gorge.

This looks straight down into the Cirque des Navacelles (below). Here, although not marked on the IGN 1:25k map, perhaps for health and safety reasons, a delicate red and white way-marked steep alternative to the plotted GR7 leaves the gorge. From the viewpoint the GR way-marks are followed eastwards down to the visitors centre and car park on the west side of the D713 road.

Navacelles from the Northern Rim of the Gorges du Vis

From there GR7 goes north just to the west of the D713 for 0.5km. Then, as the road turns to the right, the GR continues northwards on a stony path for a further 0.65km before joining the D158. A short distance right along this road the GR follows a track to the left that meanders eastwards across the plateau. Yellow way-marks are more apparent than the red and white marks, which are at best parsimoniously used on this section of GR7. The flowers on the way across the plateau are magnificent in spring. Military Orchids, with each of their florets resembling a little helmeted soldier (photo next page), are particularly plentiful in early May. Where the track splits way-marks are followed to the left and the track soon reaches the drive that leads to the Château d'Assas. The way-marked path passes through field gates on either side of the drive to the north of the chateau, unlike the route shown on the 2017 IGN map, which loops past the chateau. The path continues just north of east and makes a loop to the north before arriving at the hamlet of le Barral. Here the GR turns left and follows the lane for 0.21km before leaving through a gate to the right and continuing on a narrow grassy path between hedges. This delightful path meanders northwards, eventually becoming a track that gradually climbs to a col at 666m between two hillocks.

From the col the outline of the Cévennes north of le Vigan comes into view. Now the track winds round to the right before turning northwards again, descending to the D113 road. In May 2017 the exit to the road had been blocked, but it was easy enough to cross the fence a short way to the left.

Military Orchid

Once on the road the route heads east for a short distance and then follows a path to the left that goes north-eastwards for 1.3km before turning right onto a track, now clearly marked with red and white GR way-marks. These continue from here at regular intervals through to le Vigan. The track leads eastwards to a lane (D113a) on the outskirts of Montdardier, where the GR turns left and then takes the second turning to the right that climbs north-westwards and later northwards past a quarry. After going through a gate across the lane a right fork is taken. Then after a further 0.5km the GR leaves the road, going to the right and continuing on a way-marked path that descends through forest. At times the descent is in steep zigzags. Despite being GR7, in May 2017, this path did not appear to have been used much. A number of fallen trees across the path had to be negotiated. Notably on the descent the terrain changes to schist from the limestone of the previous days. Associated with this change sweet chestnut trees become frequent in the forest. Eventually the GR levels off, crosses a bridge and then turns left onto the D485 road that descends through the small town of Avèze.

Le Vigan lies north of Avèz and on the other side of the the River l'Arre. There is a hotel, the Auberge Cocagne, in Avèze and another, le Mas de la Prairie, on the road into la Vigan from the south. The author has stayed at both of these. He found them somewhat disappointing and expensive for the service received. Other walkers met at le Ranquas recommended a bed and breakfast lodging, the Hotel du Commerce in the centre of le Vigan (26 Rue des Barris, 30120 Le Vigan, +33 4 67 81 03 28). This seems to be a pleasant and more economical option and there are restaurants available nearby. To get to this hotel GR7 is followed northwards through Avèze. The GR then crosses a bridge over the River Arre and follows a pleasant riverside path northwards for 1.6km. It then deviates left from the river bank and continues along the Rue de la Carrierasse. After crossing a bridge over the main road a right turn into the Rue des Barris leads to the Hotel du Commerce on the left.

The climb out of le Vigan on GR68A in stormy weather

Day 5: le Vigan to Valleraugue (370m)
17.2km, up 1,318m, down 1,182m, high point the Pic de Barette 1,318m, 6h17

The walk from le Vigan climbs northwards on a broad ridge to the Pic de Barette. It then the descends the sharp eastern crête of this hill on the way to the ancient village of Valleraugue in the upper Hérault valley.

Turning left out of the hotel the street leads to the Place du Quay, which is followed downhill to a mini roundabout. The route continues just left of straight ahead into the Place d'Assas. Then the third left into the Boulvard du Plan d'Auvergne, followed by the first right, leads to the red and white way-marks of GR60A. These way-marks are followed through the northern outskirts of the town to where the GR heads steeply uphill, on a broad path from the Chemin de Gaujac. The base of this path is stony and well-drained (as can be seen above). It crosses a lane and later turns right onto a track, following this

Mountains of the Provençal Rim

briefly before heading uphill to the left and joining the D170. A short way along this mountain road to the right the GR shortcuts a hairpin bend. Then, after rejoining the road, turns left and almost at once follows a track on the left that climbs east-southeast to a telecommunications mast on a higher ridge.

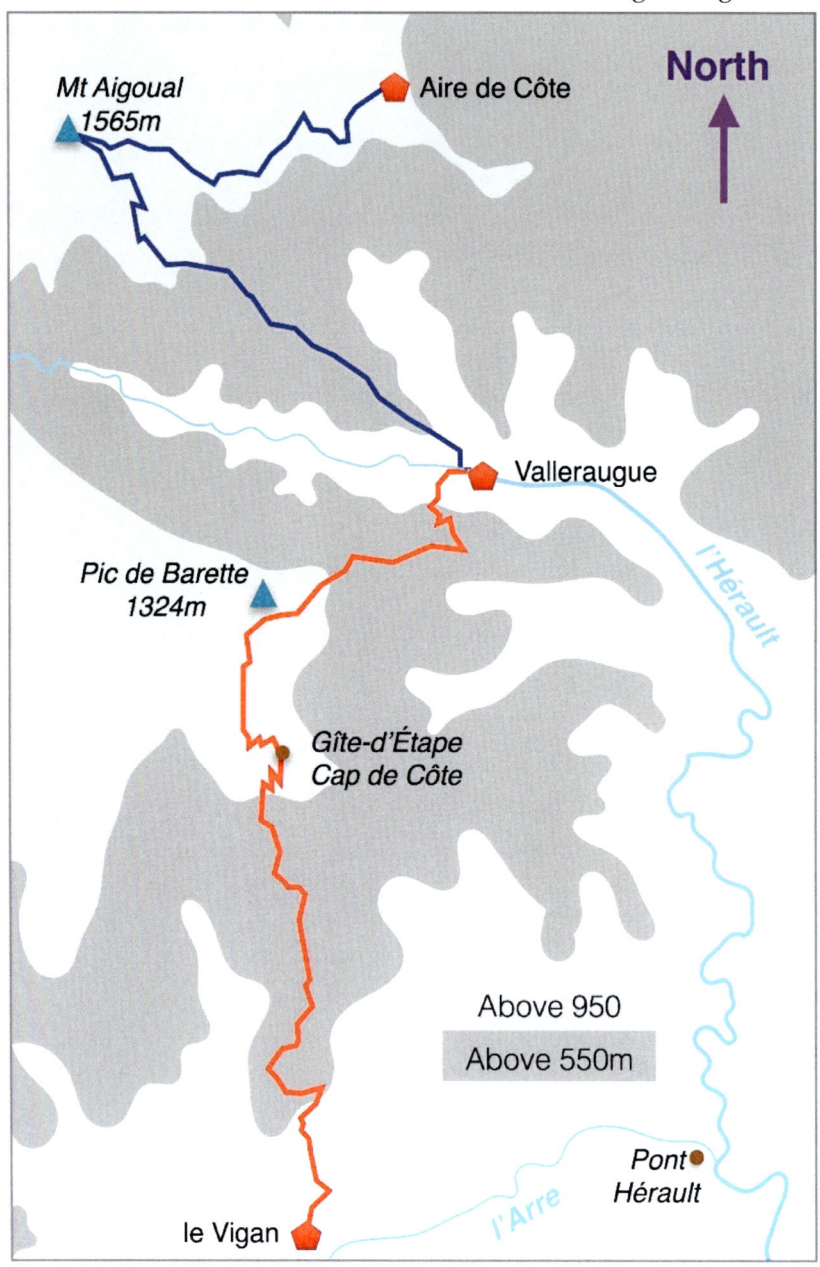

Cévennes walk days 5 and 6

From the mast, the route heads north-westwards along the ridge on a well-made narrow track. This climbs gently as it meanders from one side of the ridge to the other, with fine views to either side through gaps in the mixed woodland. At 830m the track briefly joins another lane, the D329, before climbing more steeply in zigzags to the left of the lane. The D329 is encountered twice more before the GR 60A ends at the Gîte d'Étape Cap de Côte (1189m), which lies to the left of this lane. The route then continues on a track (GR60) that zigzags uphill behind the gîte. As the gradient eases the track becomes a straight green lane that heads northwards along a broad forested ridge that tops out at 1331m.

On the final steep descent into Valleraugue

A gentle descent from this summit leads to a division of paths in a clearing, where the route turns right from GR60, once more crossing the D329 and then following GR62C towards Valleraugue. This path at first heads northwards. Then it skirts beneath the summit of the Pic de Barette (1318m) before heading down its sharp east ridge; a great walk on a fine day. At 888m the path crosses the now-wooded ridge and on the far side follows the path to Valleraugue. This is clearly marked with red and white flashes and is at first easy going, until, after a while, a right fork is followed, signed with yellow way-marks that descends much more steeply towards the village centre (above). This path reaches the road through the village near the tourist information centre.

The hotel les Bruyères www.hotelvalleraugue.com/ is down the road to the right. This period building has considerable charm and the hotel gives a warm welcome. The restaurant is excellent for hungry walkers.

Mountains of the Provençal Rim

Day 6: Valleraugue to Gîte d'Étape d'Aire de Côte (1,085m)
13.9km, up 1,560m, down 847m, high point Mt Aigoual 1,565m, 5h50

This is a memorable horseshoe walk from Valleraugue up one ridge to the summit of Mt Aigoual, the second highest hill in the Cevennes. The descent is down another ridge to the Gîte d'Étape d'Aire de Côte.

Gentle scrambling on the Sentier des Quatre Mille Marches

Up the road from the hotel the route crosses the river by the first bridge and starts along the D10 road. Soon a left turn is made into a square in front of the church. At the far end of the church waymarks lead along narrow cobbled lanes to steps that climb to the Chemin de Mangle, from where there is a good view over the red-tiled roofs of the houses in the old town. The Sentier des Quatre Mille Marches starts from the left side of the east end of this chemin and heads up the southeast ridge of Mt Aigoual. The "Marches" of this delightful footpath are Roman double paces so it is 8 rather than 4 km to the summit from Valleraugue. The footpath is of continued interest, but is in no way difficult or dangerous. The beginning of the walk climbs through chestnut forest, with several stretches involving minor scrambles up easy rocks (above). After a while the sentier emerges from forest onto an enjoyable rocky ridge and follows this until the ground steepens and the path veers to the left climbing into a hanging valley. The path crosses the stream at the base of the valley and climbs through beech woods. Several twists and zigzags later the now-much-smaller stream is again crossed and the climb skirts rocky hillside, at first heading eastwards and then going up a ridge to the north-west. When the path leaves the ridge it crosses a grassy clearing and climbs steadily to the road that circles the summit of Mt Aigoual. The high grassland to the north and west of the summit is scattered with daffodils in May (below) and there are fine views in all directions. The presence of a cafe just below the summit, perhaps provides some compensation for the invasion of the top of the hill by the motor car. Fortunately the road is only crossed just below the summit and the rest of the walk is entirely peaceful.

Wild dafodils in early May in the summit meadows of Mt Aigoual

On reaching the top of Mt Aigoual the walk joins the watershed between the Atlantic and Mediterranean. This watershed forms the line of the walk until it reaches the east end of Mt Lozère on day 9. The drainage to the left on the way down from Mt Aigoual is into the Tarnon, which joins up with the Tarn just north of Florac. The Tarn from its source on Mt Lozère flows west for 381km before reaching the Garrone. Quite why the Garrone takes precedence over the the Tarn is not clear, for although the source of the Garrone is on the Spanish side of the Pyrenees it runs a shorter course to its confluence with the Tarn.

There are two ways down to the Aire de Côte. The easier and somewhat longer route is on GR7. This is quite complex, but is adequately way-marked.

It heads east on a broad stony track from the eastern apex of the road that circles the summit of Mt Aigoual. After 0.45km the track loops to the north away from the east ridge and, on its return to the ridge, the GR leaves for a minor track along the ridge past the viewpoint at the Cap de Brion. Then this minor track also turns away from the ridge. After a further 0.6km the GR turns onto a path to the right and descends in a long loop round a wooded cirque. Eventually this path joins a well made, relatively level track that continues to the left of the east ridge to the Gîte d'Étape d'Air de Côte.

From the signpost at the Cap de Brion, near the top of the East Ridge of Mt Aigoual

The direct route to the gîte d'étape is recommended if the weather is good. This is not marked on the IGN map, but follows yellow way-marks down the east ridge of Mt Aigoual from the Cap de Brion. This way down is more scenic and although exciting in places is quite safe in good conditions. It mainly follows the edge of the ridge, but from time to time escapes into the woods to the left. The photo above looks down the east ridge from the Cap de Brion. From the crête there are fine views to the south to the rocky southeast ridge climbed in the morning and beyond that to the ridge of the Pic de Barette, which was descended the previous afternoon (above and picture page 39). In the spring, clusters of wild tulips bloom along the ridge in patches of grass among the rocks. The ridge path ends when it rejoins GR7 at le Coulet (1063m) and follows this along the broad track to the justifiably popular Gîte d'Étape d'Air de Côte. This comfortable and welcoming stopover is well worth visit www.airedecote.com.

Cévennes walk days 7 and 8

Day 7: Aire de Côte to Barre-des-Cévennes (948m)
23.0km, up 652m, down 793m, high point 1,180m just north of start, 6h00

This high level walk is mainly on GR7. It continues to follow the watershed between the Atlantic and Mediterranean. At first it goes along a broad winding ridge, before crossing open plateau to la Hospitalet. After briefly following the Corniche des Cévennes road to the Col des Faisses the GR heads east, rounding the southern end of a projection from the plateau, the Can Noire. It then descends to the ancient hill village of the Barre-des-Cévennes.

The GR7 on the IGN 1:25k map follows a track running west from the Aire de Côte, but it is preferable to follow alternative GR flashes that lead up the hill to the north-west of the gîte. After climbing 70m the way-marks head north-north-eastwards along a pleasant broad green-way through forest. The green-way joins the plotted GR7 after a little over 2km and then continues on a forest track that soon emerges onto open hillside. Now the track follows a delightful undulating ridge (below). After descending to the Col Salidès the track climbs through a sea of broom, which, when in flower, fills the air with a delicious honey-sweet nutty scent. At the top of the hill broom gives way to a meadow filled with wild tulips in the spring (photo page 62). These meadows continue to the col des Marquairès. Now the geology changes, passing from schist back again to limestone.

The delightful undulating ridge before the Col Salidès and the sea of broom

The continuation heads northwards to the right of impressive ragged limestone cliffs that fall to beech woods in the valley of the Tarnon. On reaching the Hospitalet the route follows the Cornish des Cévennes road for a short distance to the Col des Faisses. From there the GR heads right on a red-orange sandy track that crosses the Can Noire, a flat-topped promontory that extends to the east of the cornish. There are fine views from here north to Mont Lozère. On reaching the southeast edge of the promontory GR7 descends on a path to a track that circles anticlockwise round the escarpment to the D983 road, which is followed eastwards into the Barre-des-Cévennes. At the far end of the long narrow main street of the village a left fork leads to the Gîte d'Étape la Croisette, which is situated on the far side of the next road junction. This is another welcoming stopover. The dining room walls are decorated with stuffed heads of wild boar and various deer. When the author stayed there he was served with several protein-rich courses of locally acquired game. This gîte does not seem to have a web-site, but can be booked by 'phone 33 (0)4 66 45 05 28.

Day 8: Barre-des-Cévennes to Vieljouvès-Bas (932m)
24.3km, up 993m, down 1,010m, high point 1,100m, 6h50

Most of this walk continues on GR7 following forest tracks that run along broad high ridges. After climbing to the summit of la Cayla there is a descent to the Col de Jalcreste, the high point on the main road between Alès and Florac. From there the route deviates from GR7 to reach the isolated Eco-Gîte de Vieljouvès.

The monument at the Plan de Fontmort

For the first km the GR7/67 follows the D13 mountain road along a broad ridge, maintaining height between 950 and 1,000m. After a while the GR continues on paths that run first on one side of the road and then the other. Some 5km from the Barre-des-Cévennes the road splits at the Plan de Fontmort. A stone memorial (above) stands at this junction. It marks the century of religious tolerance that followed the war of the Camisards, which afflicted the people of the Cévennes at the beginning of the 18th century. This war was provoked by King Louis XIV's Edict of Fontainebleau (1685), which sadly cancelled his grandfather, King Henry IV's, Edict of Nantes of (1598). The Edict of Nantes had allowed a high degree of religious freedom in France during the previous century and had put an end to the terrible religious wars that raged in France in the late 16th century. Following the Edict of Fontainebleau there was renewed persecution of the protestant Huguenots with mass deportation, forced conversions and the sacking of several villages in the Cévennes. This led to reprisals starting with the murder of the Abbé du Chaila at le Pont de Montvert. During the next 2 years the protestant Camisards conducted a successful guerrilla campaign in the Cévennes against royal catholic forces. Louis XIV may be known as the sun king, but his reign was not all sunshine.

Wild tulips on the Atlantic-Mediterranean watershed

From the monument GR7/67 runs eastwards between the two roads ascending gradually on a track on the south face of wooded hillside. After 0.5km GR70, alias the Stevenson Trail, joins from the left. The combined GRs continue to climb on the track to a clearing where there is a fine view south, past a menhir (standing stone) to Mt Aigoual. Here the tracks divide. GR70 leaves to the right while our route continues on GR7/67, now a broad track that climbs gently through forest to the high point of the day, which is marked by a cairn. The route then heads northeastwards downhill from the cairn on a path through forest. This leads to a grassy clearing at the Col des Laupies, a junction of several tracks and paths. From there GR7/67 initially heads north on a sandy forest road. This road runs on the left side of a wooded ridge. Soon it winds round to the east and eventually GR7 leaves the track and heads uphill to the right on a narrower track that leads to the Col des Abeilles. Now GR7 climbs to the left up an open ridge to the summit of le Cayla, leaving GR67, which traverses to the right. The descent from le Cayla starts along the northwest ridge following GR7. After a while the path veers onto the northeastern flank of the ridge and becomes a schist pavement in the last section before the main road at the col de Jalcreste. Turning left on the road in the direction of Florac the route leaves GR7 and descends for a short distance until a small road is followed to the right towards the village of le Rouve Bas. The road then climbs west to a col where a right turn onto a narrow lane leads up the Vieljouvès valley.

The Eco-Gîte de Vieljouvès and Dominique van Waddingen

This lane climbs through one hairpin before descending past a farm. Eventually the lane crosses the valley stream and climbs in long zigzags to the hamlet of Vieljouvès-Bas, where the last house is the delightful Eco-gîte de Vieljouvès   http://www.cevennes-gite.eu/index.php?static1/gite-d-etape (above with the owner Dominique van Weddingen). Unlike the previous protein-rich evening meal the repast in Dominiques living room at the eco-gîte was vegetarian.

Mountains of the Provençal Rim

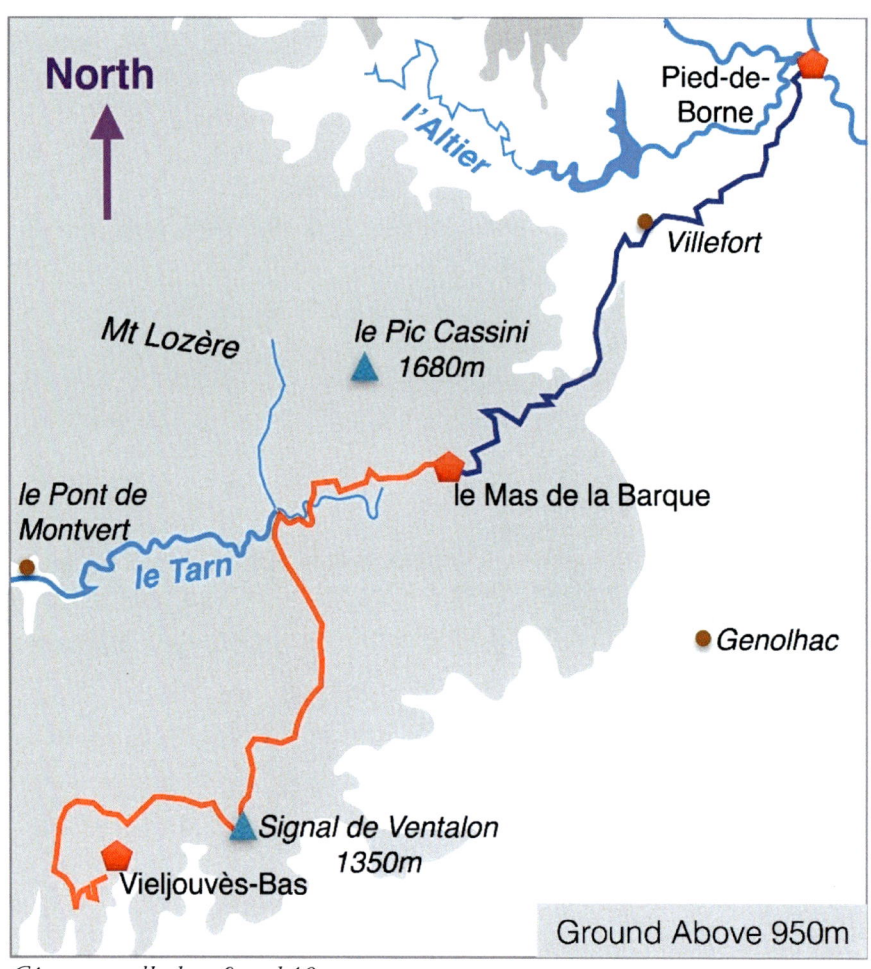

Cévennes walk days 9 and 10

Day 9: Vieljouvès-Bas to le Mas de la Barque (1,417m)
25.3km, up 1,148, down 669m, high point 1,437m Senegriere, 7h20

This fine high-level walk climbs to the Signal de Ventalon, the high point of the Montaigne du Bouges. After descending to the Croix de Berthel the route climbs again to the east end of Mt Lozere. Dominique suggests the route given below that joins up with GR67 on the way to the Signal de Ventallon. This is marked with black dashes on IGN maps rather than the magenta of official footpaths and is strongly recommended.

The lane and then track are followed up to the houses at Vieljouvès-Haut. In front of the stone buildings the track peters out and the route continues south along the edge of the field behind the last house. From there a path is followed southwards. This is at first indistinct but soon improves, continuing to a crossing of paths. A right turn here, onto a grassy path leads uphill, east-north-eastwards, to a track, which is followed to the right, north-north-eastwards. It may be necessary here to push aside broom that has fallen across this track. The track winds round to the south and eventually reaches a fine view point. From there the route follows the track north-north-westwards and climbs to a broader track on the Pierre Courbe Ridge. This leads up to GR72, which is followed eastwards along or just below the broad undulating ridge of the Montagne du Bouges.

Looking across to the east end of Mont Mt Lozère from the Signal de Ventalon

Eventually the track climbs to the summit, the Signal de Ventalon (1,350m) where GR7 joins GR72. To the north lies the east end of Mt Lozère (above). Southwards runs the watershed ridge walked along during the previous days, which leads to Mt Aigoual. The descent northwards goes along a broad firebreak to the road at the Croix de Berthel (1,088m). On the far side of the croix GR7/72 is followed northwards along a track. For a while this gradually winds round to the east and then slowly curves back to the north. Just as the track again starts to turn eastwards the combined GR leaves, climbing northeastwards along a firebreak. At 1,285m it comes out of the forest and heads down an ancient stone-paved path through a delightful field strewn with granite boulders. This path leads across a fine stone bridge to the farm at l'Aubaret.

On the far side of the bridge the GR continues past the farm climbing, at first northwards and then northwestwards between boulders. There are plenty of way-marks, but these are not very accurately placed and some care is needed

Mountains of the Provençal Rim

to follow the route. After climbing to 1,350m the path levels off and continues on a wide grassy swathe through forest before descending to the Pont du Tarn. This great southern French river has impressive gorges further downstream, but at this stage is still relatively small.

Crossing the Vérié

Instead of crossing the bridge on GR7 our route follows GR72 eastwards on a well-made grit track that runs through forest, south of the river. Where the track loops for the second time to the south GR72 heads northwards on a path towards a tributary of the Tarn, the Vérié. Here the river crossing is a wade (above), as there is neither a bridge nor stepping stones. The river is about 8m wide, but even in late spring after snow melt the water was no more than knee deep and the bottom of granite sand kind to the feet[1]. On the far side the path crosses fields to reach the largely-abandoned hamlet of Bellecoste. The quality of the granite walls and lintels of its ancient buildings is impressive. After continuing from Bellecost eastwards on GR72 for about 2km the track enters

---

[1] In the event of difficulty following GR72 across the river, continue on the track south of the river that was followed from the Pont du Tarn. This links up with the stony road going from Bellecoste to the Mas de la Barque and is only about half a km longer than the wading route. Note, there is no obvious path or track between the north side of the Pont du Tarn and Bellecoste.

sparse woodland and a similar distance further on reaches le Mas de la Barque. Here there are a number of buildings to the right of the track. The Gîte d' Étape le Mas de la Barque lies at the southeast end of the complex http://www.lemasdelabarque.com/. This comfortable gîte has a good bar-restaurant. It is well worth a visit and is good value for money.

Gnarled Beaches at 1400m on Mont Lozère

Day 10: le Mas de la Barque to Pied-de-Borne (328m)
23.9km, up 619m, down 1,711m, high point 1,449m east of le Mas, 6h00

The descent from the Mas follows GR72 eastwards on a track through beech woods, where the harsh conditions have produced characterful gnarled specimens (above). After descending some 80m GR72 follows a path north-westwards and then to the northeast that climbs back to the high point of the day on the road running from the Mas de la Barque to Villefort. After walking back towards the mas along the road for about 0.1km the GR heads off into the forest on the right and leads on an uncertain path to the road that descends to Villefort. Some 0.3km down this road GR72 heads diagonally back to the right on a well-made grassy track. This track traverses steep forested hillside to a point above the open northeast-running ridge that leads towards Villefort. Here the route continues on a zigzagging path down through the forest before meeting another track that descends through one hairpin bend to the start of the ridge. At first the GR goes over a series of granite tors on the ridge with some easy scrambling at one point. In places broom intrudes onto the path. After about a km the path descends to a stony track that leads along the open ridge for a further 3km. When the track reaches forest, it descends steeply and there are views on the left to the lake on the north side of Villefort, formed by damming the River Altier. On reaching a col the GR follows a broad forest track to the right that gently descends in multiple zigzags, until it reaches the south-western outskirts of Villefort. There it continues on a paved lane to the main north-south road, where a left turn leads under the railway. Then the second turning on the right, followed almost immediately by a further right turn, leads to a square with a fountain. The road leading east from the square curves to the right, continuing above a stream, with well-tended vegetable plots on the far side below a row of houses.

The east end of Mt Lozère from below the Chapelas Roc telecommunications station

    Soon the road turns left across a bridge and on the far side the route continues up the road to the right. This road becomes a track that climbs through many zigzags to the Chapelas Roc telecommunications station at the top of the hill. In spring flowers along the track are abundant and there are fine views back to Mt Lozère and the ridge followed earlier in the day (above). The route passes to the south of the telecom. station before descending gently to a sandy track that traverses north across the east side of the hill. The track, GR du Payes: Tour du Chassezac, leads to a broad col, where at a signpost the GR is followed to the left on a path that winds down to the village of les Salces. This ancient path is made with a stone base, providing even walking down the steep hillside that forms the south-eastern wall of the impressive gorge of the torrential river Altier. The noise of its cascading water becomes ever more apparent on the approach les Salces. From the village a pleasant lightly-shaded lane leads to the simple hotel at Pied-de-Borne – Les Gorges du Chassezac +33

4 66 462553 http://www.hotellerie-du-chassezac-lozere.com/ . This hostelry is very much the village bar used by the locals and itinerant workers from projects associated with the hydroelectric scheme at Pied-de-Borne. The accommodation is comfortable and the food plentiful in this affordable stopover

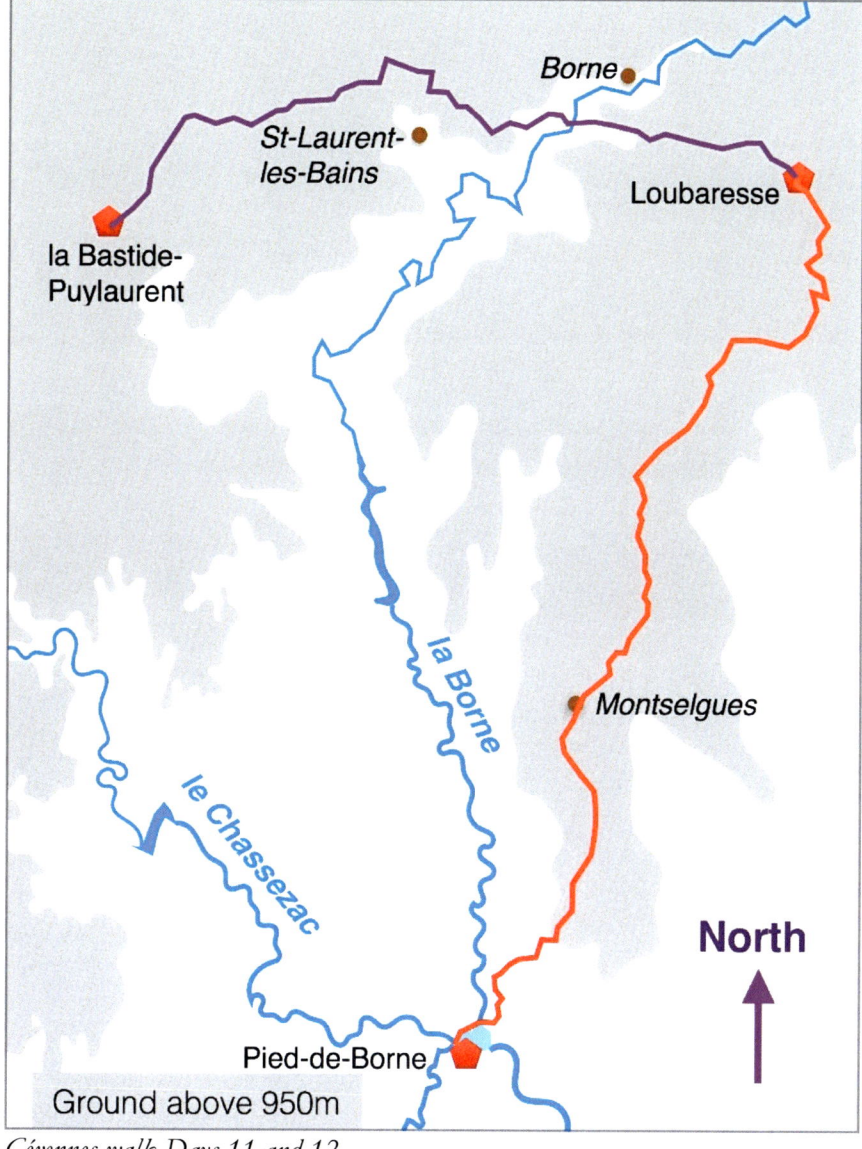

Cévennes walk Days 11 and 12

Pied-de-Borne from Sainte Marguerite Lafigère

Day 11: Pied-de-Borne to Loubaresse (1,210m)
21.5km, up 1,369m, down 501m, high point 1,210m Loubaresse, 8h00

Pied-de-Borne (above) is situated at the meeting of 3 rivers – the Borne, the Altier and the Chassezac. These flow into a lake formed by a hydroelectricity dam and the river below the barrage is the Chassezac. Each or these rivers reaches the confluence through an impressive deep gorge. Above the Pied-de-Borne is the hill village of Planchamp, which has at least 3 churches and on the far side of the barraged lake another village – Sainte-Marguerite-Lafigère, also has a church.

After crossing the Bridge over the merged Altier and Chassezac the route continues on the narrow road round the back of the hydroelectric station and across a bridge where the Borne flows into the lake. The Borne here forms the boundary between the Lozere and the Ardeche regions. Soon the road up the east side of the Borne valley branches off to the left. Rather than take this, head up a narrow metaled lane that rises from the far side of this road. The lane soon becomes a grassy track that zigzaggs up to a higher narrow lane.

Heading northwards the top lane leads past the old stone church of Sainte-Marguerite-Lafigère with its two external bells. After this the lane joins the lower road and continues up the east side of the Borne Valley. On reaching the hamlet of le Pont the route turns right onto a lane that climbs past the houses to a path signed as the Sainte Marguerite Circuit. This path is not marked on the IGN map, but yellow way-marks make it easy to follow. At a water mill it continues climbing, crossing a horizontal path along the aqueduct that goes to le Soulie. The circuit path zigzags through steep chestnut coppice (below) to the top of the escarpment. It is important to follow the way-marks near the top, where there is some easy scrambling. Eventually the path reaches a track that runs along the edge of the escarpment. On the far side a weathered signpost indicates an overgrown path that leads eventually to the ancient village of Montselgues. Pushing aside the broom, follow this path climbing to the ruins of a granite house. From there turn right and soon reach a track. Turn left onto this and follow it through forest to a row of electricity pylons and continue beside these north-eastwards to a broad sandy road. The route then follows this road northwards away from the pylons and on to Montselgues.

On the Ste Marguerite Circuit above le Pont

From this village the route heads northeast on GR du Payes: Tour de la Montagne Ardèchoise. This crosses a broom-covered hillside at over 1,000m to the hamlet of la Borie where it joins GR4. The GR is followed northwards as it climbs uphill, shortcutting the lane that serves the cluster of houses grandly named – Petit Paris. Once past these the path continues climbing up the broad ridge of the Serre de l'Estelle. As the climb eases the path crosses open hillside, again covered with broom. The path passes to the right of the farmstead at les Cayres before going through a small gate and reaching a lane. The GR heads right along the lane and soon joins the D4 road, continuing left on this for some

Mountains of the Provençal Rim

0.1km before going through another small wooden gate to the right. Now a signpost (below) indicates the continuation of GR4 towards Loubaresse on a grassy path to the left that heads north-eastwards downhill. After joining a stony track and then crossing a small stream the GR climbs on the track through meadow with exceptional narcissi and broom. Soon the track enters woodland and then follows a shallow gully with plates of red schist underfoot. As the gully floor rises to the level of the surrounding forest the track gradually works its way round to the north ascending to join the D403 at a bend in this road. Almost immediately GR4 leaves the road again on a track that heads north-north-eastwards reaching the rim of the deep valley of the River Drobie, which falls to the right. After following the rim round to the east for a while the red

Broom-covered hillside on the way to Loubaresse

and white way-marks again lead north-eastwards away from the edge and descend through the forest. When some 100m height has been lost GR4 once more joins the D403 just before a hairpin bend. From here it is not far along the road to the destination for the night, but purists might want to follow the footpath as it follows a somewhat artificial course first above the right side of the road and then below its left edge. Loubaresse is an attractive, small and sleepy hill village that is happily bypassed by the road. There is a bar/restaurant at its centre. Accommodation is available at the Gîte d'Étape de Loubaresse http://www.gitedeloubaresse-ardeche.fr/contact.php .

Day 12: Loubaresse to la Bastide-Puylaurent (1,016m)
17.1km, up 757m, 938m down, high point 1,264m the Coulet de Pécovol, 5h34

After the long previous day the final walk is comparatively easy. In the village there is a small épicerie (below) where something can be brought for lunch. The walk heads west out of the village on a GR de Pays: Tour de la Montagne Ardéchoise. This soon joins a lane that leads to the village of Borne, which lies at the base of the Gorges de la Borne. The GR shortcuts a couple of hairpin bends in the lane and then leaves it to the left, descending westwards through forest losing some 400m before reaching the river Borne.

The store in Lubaresse

Across the bridge the footpath climbs steeply and joins our old friend GR72 some 90m above the river.[2] Turning left onto the GR the route climbs gradually to the west through forest. After a while the path comes onto open ground and climbs steeply in zigzags to a col at just over 1000m. Ignore the GR which descends from here through forest to the small spar town of Saint-Laurent-les-Bains and follow a track north-westwards from the col that climbs up the ridge to the right. After 0.2k the track splits and the right-hand, upper

---

[2] GR72 arrives here from Villefort having followed a line close to the main north-south road to la Bastide-Puylaurent

branch is followed that heads just north of west. The track climbs gently and steadily round the large, south-facing cirque, high above St Laurent. Eventually the western rim of the cirque is reached at the Coulet de Pécovol (1,264m). The photograph below looks down on St Laurent from the hillside just east of this coulet. The track the route takes to the coulet is the less-distinct upper of the two tracks that can be seen crossing the hillside above and to the left of Saint-Laurent.

Above Saint-Larent-les Bains

At the coulet the track crosses GR7 and continues on the far side just south of west through forest on a minor track that is also marked on a tree as cycle route 49. The route continues on this track as it winds between the tops of an elongated, broad east-west forested ridge known as the Sommet de la Felgère. At first this narrow track is pleasantly-shaded and descends gently before flattening out. It becomes grassy as it passes to the north of the first summit of the ridge. At the far end of this summit the track crosses the ridge and again descends gently. A larger track joins from the left and soon there is a further junction of tracks. Here our route follows the path that heads westwards marked on a signpost to Rogleton and the Sommet d'Espervelouze. This is labelled as cycle track 27 and has yellow and white way-marks. As the track climbs gently on the south side of the Sommet de la Felgère the Trappist monastery "Notre Dame des Neiges" can be seen below and to the left through the trees. This was one of the places, where Robert Louis Stevenson stopped during his 19th century 'Travels with a Donkey through the Cévennes'. The track continues to the Sommet d'Espervelouze (1,225m), which is an open grassy dome decorated with a large electricity pylon. Despite this intrusion there are magnificent views from the summit; south across the Cévennes, westwards to the Allier valley and northwards (below) to the distant summits of the Ardeche volcanoes topped by Mont Mezenc. In late May the nutty-honey scent of broom at the Sommet d'Espervelouze is everywhere and its blooms glow golden in sunny weather. From this last summit the route heads southwest, descending steeply on a stony track (still cycle track 27, but now carrying red and yellow way-marks). La Bastide-Pylaurent can be seen far below in the direction of the track. At first the way is down the broom-clad open hillside, but as the descent eases it enters forest and continues southwestwards. After passing to the right of a large building, the track joins a lane and GR7, with its red and white way-marks. This lane continues south-westwards and leads to the final destination in the village of la Bastide-Puylaurent.

Looking north from last summit on the walk through the Cévennes

In the middle of the village on the west side of the main north-south road between Langong and Alès lies the Hotel la Grand Halt http://www.labastide-hotel.com. This is a convenient stopover for the last night. It is named after the junction of minor rail lines on the far side of the village. The trains from here still go north up the valley of the Allier to Clermont Ferrand, west to Mend and South to Alès. In the 19th century, apart from being an important railway junction la Bastide-Puylaurent was the stop for the fashionable spar at St Laurent les Bains. The motor car and perhaps a modest increase in scepticism for the benefits of taking the waters has reduced the throng of visitors, but la Bastide-Puylaurent remains a good place to start or finish a long walk.

Mountains of the Provençal Rim

Broom, sorrel and thrift seen from GR4 near Loubaresse day 11

4 CHAPTER
HIGH RIDGES OF THE DIOIS HILLS
An 8 day circular walk from Die of 161.6km, with 10,294m ascent

Although a significant centre in Roman times and a cathedral city from the fourth century Die was robbed of its bishopric during the French Revolution and became absorbed into the diocese of Grenoble. It might now be described as a provincial French town that is best known for its delicious sparkling wine. The trouble is that few people outside the region are familiar with this refreshing drink. All of this obscurity is a distinct advantage for the hill walker, who wishes to explore the hills that rise on either side of the Drôme valley. To the north the cliffs of the Vercors escarpment rise more than 1,500m above the town, while to the south are a series of high limestone ridges and stand-alone peaks set on top of steep wooded hillside and fertile valleys. When the author did this walk in early June 2014 the flowers on the hills were at their magnificent best and the weather was hot, so any shade was welcome. Although the neighbouring tops and gullies in the Dévoluy and Vercors still had some snow the Diois hills, even at their high point of 1700m, were clear. The considerable distance between some of the stopovers on this walk reflects the remoteness of these fine hills and the wide spacing of villages. The sparseness of other walkers adds to the charm of this tour.

Summary of the Diois Hills walk

Day 1: Die to Rimon (1010m)
20.4km, up 1,529m, down 965m, high point Montagne de Beaufayn 1,251m, 7h09

Day 2: Rimon to St-Nazaire-le-Désert (580m)
18.1km, up 770m, down 1,166m, high point Rochers des Blaches 1,009m, 5h31

Day 3: St-Nazaire to Ferme St Antoine near la Motte-Chalancon (670m)
18.9km, up 1,038m, down 936m, high point le Grand Désert 1,115m, 6h00

Day 4: Ferme St Antoine to Valdrôme (789m)
24.0km, up 1,675m, down 1,535m, high point Montagne de Tarsimoure 1,556m, 9h00

Day 5: Valdrôme to Saint-Pierre-d'Argençon (785m)
22.8km, up 1,512m, down 1,529m, high point le Pyramide 1,735m, 8h50

Day 6: Saint-Pierre-d'Argençon to le Pilhon (1,086m)
16.8km, up 1,357m, down 1,053m, high point the Banne 1,643m, 6h10

Day 7: Le Pilhon to Châtillon-en-Diois (570m)
21.3km, up 1,060m, down 1,556m, high point Col du Roi 1,369m, 6h50

Day 8: Châtillon-en-Diois to Die (396m)
19.3, up 1353m, down 1,556m, high point Montagne de Label 1,173m, 7h00

Total 161.6km, 10,294m ascent; average 20.2km, 1,287m ascent

Les Trois Becs from le Col les Vignes on the morning of day 3

High ridges of the Diois hills

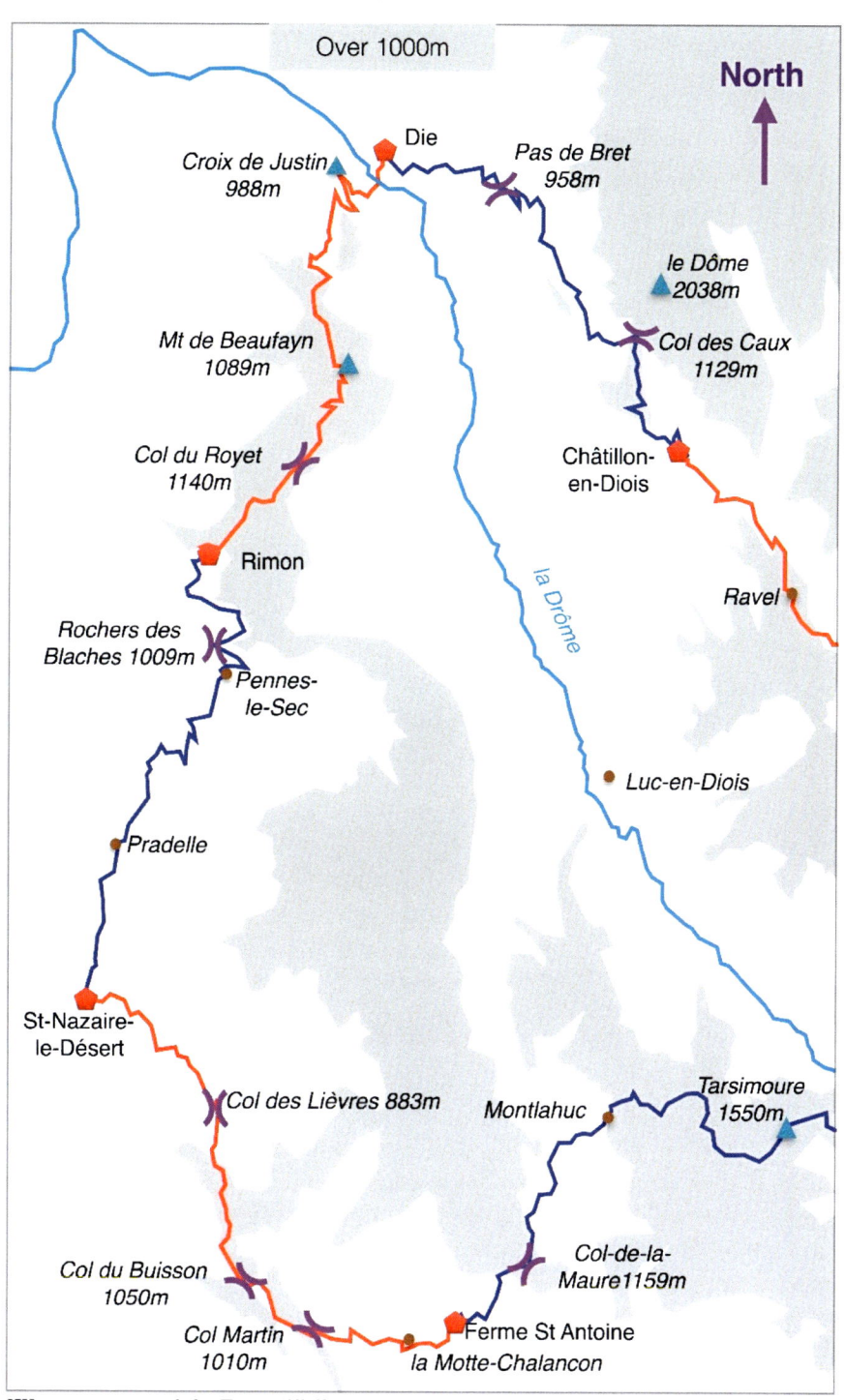

Western stages of the Diois Hills walk

Journey to Die

As on the Die to Briançon walk (Chapter 2) the start is reached by train from Lyon. Once more the Petit Auberge lapetiteauberge.com, conveniently set across the road from the station, provides a comfortable stay at the beginning and end of this walk.

Day 1: Die to Rimon (1010m)
20.4km, up 1,529m, down 965m, high point Pas du Loup 1,251m, 7h09

The hills rise steeply on the south side of the Drôme, providing a good workout at the start of the walk before reaching the first viewpoint, the Croix du Justin. Then the route provides continued interest as it proceeds to Rimon.

The limestone outcrop topped by the Croix du Justin from the southern outskirts of Die

The eastward start from the auberge follows the roads along the railway as it loops to the south between the old town and the river. From the main road a right turn into the Chemin de la Recluse leads past the cemetery and continues to the junction with the Boulevard des Ursulines. The first right into the Chemin du Pont Giraud leaves the traffic and continues peacefully down to a bridge over the railway. On the far side, the Chemin du Pont Rompu leads to a footbridge over the River Drôme where the route joins GR95, which is followed for most of the day. Beyond the river the GR winds up the escarpment to the Croix du Justin. At 673m the path divides, providing two options to reach the croix. The right fork, still GR95, makes a long westwards traverse before doubling back and climbing gradually to a rough road at a hairpin bend. After about 0.1km a path heads back uphill, shortcutting a loop in the road. Once back on the road the route follows this westwards up to the croix. From there the massive cliffs of the southern Vercors escarpment dominate the view across the valley.

From the croix the route returns to a fork in the track where GR 95 turns to the right and then, almost immediately, right again onto a grassy track that descends just west of south. After the track flattens out it becomes a path that leads to the edge of a cirque surrounded by limestone cliffs. The onward path is set spectacularly, but safely, into the wall of the cliff to the left and climbs clockwise, eventually reaching the top of the cirque. It then winds through scrub above the cliff to a gîte forestière, were there is the opportunity to rest on a pleasantly, shaded bench.

The vertiginous path from the Pas du Corbeau

The route, still GR95, now heads south-south-eastwards on a track that contours round the hillside for half a km before following a path that climbs to the right, rising to a grassy ridge. The path heads south-westwards up this ridge and as it passes through 1000m starts to traverse southwards, rising gently to another ridge at the Pas du Corbeau. Here the path crosses the ridge below a rocky spur and then contours vertiginously, but securely, across a rock-face (above) on its way to the wooded Col de Beaufayn. From this col a good path climbs steeply through beech woods on the left side of the elongated Montagne de Beaufayn. After a while the path levels off before it climbs in short steep zigzags to the Pas du Loup and the floral plateau-top of the montagne. A bench here provides a comfortable lunch-stop. It is worth making a short detour to the west summit of the mountain. From this belvedere the view north looks back across the cirque to the Croix du Justin, some 250m below.

GR95 continues southwards from the Pas du Loup on a track that descends gradually through sparse coniferous forest to a junction of routes and then follows the same bearing towards the Col du Royet. After emerging onto a floral meadow the track winds to the left before passing a building and then heading once more to the south. Just before the col the track approaches the west side of the ridge of the Serre Chauvière. From the Col du Royet it is worth following the footpath running parallel to GR95 southwards along the crest of this grassy, beautifully-flowered ridge. After a while the east side of the ridge becomes precipitous at the Rochers du Baux and a line of squat conifers protects the crest of the cliff. Leave the ridge where the trees end and return diagonally downhill to the track and GR95, continuing south-westwards through flower-filled meadows. In the background lie the impressive cliffs of les Trois Becs. These form the precipitous eastern wall of the Forêt de Saou; The forest that lies to the north of the village of Saou and is encircled by an impressive 29km-long ring of limestone cliffs.

A lesser spotted woodpecker chick keeping an eye on things

Some 3km after the Col du Royet the track passes across an unnamed col and then descends to the hill village of Rimon. To reach the lodgings turn left at the top of the village and left again into the lane that runs below the Church. At the end of this lane lies the old farmhouse, labelled as Ferm des Roches on the IGN map. This is now the Gîte d'Étape la Grange au Volets Blue (blue shutters) http://gite-drome-la-grange.com/nuit.html +33 4 7521 0109 or +33 6 8952 9910. Daniel and Stéphanette Marce run this delightful gîte, but do not live there. They farm rabbits near Die and Stéphanette drives up the 30 odd km to Rimon to look after people who have booked to stay in the Gîte. When the author stayed there he was welcomed with tea and drank this on the delightful terrace. After hot showers, as he hung out his laundry in the garden, a lesser spotted woodpecker chick watched critically from a hole in the trunk of a nearby old ash tree (above). Dinner, not surprisingly, was a fine rabbit stew.

High ridges of the Diois hills

Day 2: Rimon to St-Nazaire-le-Désert (580m)
18.1km, up 770m, down 1,166m, high point Rochers des Blaches 1,009m, 5h31

This walk continues to head in a generally southerly direction to the ancient and remote village of St-Nazaire-le-Désert. It starts along the lane from the gîte and before the church follows GR95 on a path to the left. This shortcuts a long loop in the road that winds down from Rimon to the Roanne Valley. On joining this road lower down leave GR95, which continues on the far side and follow the road downhill until just before the next hairpin bend. Then a left turn to the east onto a fine path, the GR du Payes (GRP): Tour de la Vallée de la Roanne, contours round a large, thinly-forested cirque. Despite the steep walls of the cirque the path is safe and there are plenty of flowers along the path in early summer, including a number of exquisite bee orchids.

Les Rochers Blaches from the path, just before it crosses the ridge

After the apex of the cirque the path splits and the route takes the left fork, climbing gently through beech woods to a pass across a rocky ridge. The photo above looks past les Rochers Blaches from just below this pass and shows the steepness of the head of the cirque. From the pass the path descends gradually south-eastwards to a lane, the D595. Here a right turn along the lane shortcuts the GRP. After 0.5km a left turn is taken towards Pennes-le-Sec and then a turn to the right rejoins the GRP, passing to the west of the village on a lane that soon becomes a track. This heads south-south-westwards down the hill, eventually joining a forest track. Almost immediately after this junction the route turns right from both the track and the GRP onto a path along a firebreak. After a while the path turns left (west-southwest) from the fire break, descending through sparse forest, in zigzags to the east bank of the River Roanne. After crossing a side stream the path climbs up a grassy ramp to a hairpin bend on the D140. A short way down this lane it joins the valley road, the D135. South of the road junction the Roanne flows in the bottom of an impressive ravine. Our route follows the road up the western lip of this developing gorge. At the first hairpin bend, a short detour on a path to the left from the road leads to a fine viewpoint some 50m above a bend in the river.

Inspecting the fireplace in the Auberge du Désert

Returning to the road this starts to contour above the gorge at around 500m. Eventually the road passes through the village of Pradelle and some way beyond this crosses the river and continues south to the Pas du Loup. There the route leaves the road for an unclassified lane that runs along the east bank of the river into St-Nazaire. This is followed through to the south end of the village, where there is a square on the left of the lane, with the Auberge-du-Désert, http://www.auberge-du-desert.com/topic/index.html an attractive old stone building at the top of the square. This is a comfortable and modestly priced stopover for walkers. Satisfying meals are served in the dining room, where there is a massive stone fireplace (above).

Day 3: St-Nazaire to the Ferme St Antoine (670m)
18.9km, up 1,038m, down 936m, high point le Grand Désert 1,115m, 6h00

The walk sets off on GRP: Tour de la Vallée Roanne up a steep alleyway on the south side of the hotel. This leads first past the church, which has a striking group of 3 statues perched on top of the extended gable-end above two bells. Further up the lane joins the D135 road and passes the fire station. A path on the far side of this road links to a lane, the D271, which is followed to the right shortcutting the GRP and leading south-eastwards to the Col les Vignes. There are distant views from the lane of the rock towers of the Trois Becs (photograph on page 78). The route continues on the lane past the col until just before the farm at Febie (798m), where a track is taken to the left that soon links with the GRP. This then climbs south-south-eastwards to the Col des Lièvres (886m). From the col the route leaves the GRP and follows an itinéraire equestre, marked with blue dashes on the IGN map, southwards up a broad ridge. This climbs gradually over 2.9km to 1115m. Here the main track follows the ridge to the left, but our route descends on the itinéraire equestre to the right on a stoney track that leads to the D627 at the Col de Chamauche. On the descent the profile of Mt Ventoux is seen to the south. The itinéraire equestre crosses the road and follows a track that skirts round a hillock before climbing south-eastwards to the Col du Buisson.

A project for restoration at the Col Martin

On the far side of this col a steep stony path leads down to a lane that passes the les Bertrands farmstead. Just before the farm buildings a track to the left is followed that heads south-south-eastwards on the left side of a broad pasture climbing gradually to the Col Martin (above) where the remains of a rusted ancient motor car have been parked. At the col the track turns to the left and immediately splits. The left fork, still the itinéraire equestre, leads south-eastwards climbing through scrubby woodland to a pass across the Montagne de Longue Serre at 1,082m. Beyond the col the itinéraire equestre becomes a footpath that continues, descending quite steeply, at first through forest and then open country to la Motte-Chalancon. On the descent there are fine views to the hills beyond this town (below).

The descent to la Motte-Chalancon

The lodging for the night is some way to the far side of la Motte Chalancon. About 0.8km after leaving this town on the D61 a path is taken to the left from the road. The climb of 150m to the Ferme de St Antoine from the road is little more than a km, but it feels further at the end of a long hot day. This excellent equestrian and walker gîte d'étape is run by the characterful Francine Jouve http://www.lamottechalancon.com/tourisme/hebergements/gites-etape.html. The author and his walking colleagues had a memorable evening with Francine feasting on one of the farm's large guinea fowls

Day 4: La Ferme St Antoine to Valdrôme (789m)
24.0km, up 1,675m, down 1,535m, high point le Tarsimoure 1,556m, 9h00

From the farm the route heads north-eastwards on a broad unsurfaced road that winds up to a plateau. It then continues as a sandy track past the east side of an airstrip. Immediately after the track turns acutely to the left a right turn is taken onto a stony path that climbs steeply north-eastwards through forest to the Col de la Maure (1,159m). The descent from the col is on a path through woods to a dirt track. A short distance to the left the first track to the right leads gradually down to the D61 road.

After heading northwards on this road for 1.2km a right turn is taken onto a track that climbs through fields and small patches of woodland winding its way east-north-eastwards up to the village of Montlahuc. At the north end of the village the route turns right onto a track. Soon a left fork climbs eastwards in long zigzags into forest. After climbing for some 3.5km it reaches the Col de Fond Sauvage at 1,307m. Here the track ends and a right turn across a small clearing leads to a path that winds round again to the east and climbs to a wooded ridge at 1,346m. The path divides here and a further right turn heads gently downhill to the south, before climbing to the southern end of a rocky outcrop, the Grand Surnom (1,449m). The path to the summit of the rock is overgrown and the views from there are excelled by those from the Tarsimoure,

Wild Peonies on the Montage de Tarsimoure

so continue on the path southwards and then south-eastwards eventually descending to the Col de la Caille (1,299). Here there is a junction of 5 paths and the path going due east is taken. This forks after a further 0.2km. The left branch provides a safe quick route to the Col de St Pierre, but the path to right leads to a truly magnificent, if somewhat delicate, traverse of the Montagne de Tarsimoure. If you have a head for heights take the right branch and climb with the aid of fixed ropes to the rocky summit crest at 1,550m. In June the grassy east side of the crest sports an exceptional array of flowers including impressive drifts of pink peonies (above).

Looking north-eastwards along the Tarsimoure ridge

The ridge is followed north-eastwards (above) to a dip, where a path goes off to the right, providing a safe escape route that traverses back to the hamlet of les Bascoux. A notice here correctly warns that the route ahead along the ridge gets tricky. Heading northwards, the ridge climbs to 1,505m and then descends steadily. After losing 200m the ridge becomes wooded and the path deviates to the left side of the ridge, becoming distinctly steep as it winds down to the Col St Pierre (1,092m). There is no protection on the descent, other than the odd tree trunk, so it should not be attempted by the fainthearted, or in muddy conditions.

Once at the col a broad level forest track leads southwards to the Col Layard and then onwards south-eastwards. Continue on the forest track, where a marked path climbs to the right. The track winds steadily down towards Valdrôme. providing a fast, pleasant finish to a long hard day's walk. On arriving at the D106 road a right turn before a bridge leads to the Gîte d'Étape le Tarsimoure. This is a pleasant stopover that has a large garden and provides comfortable rooms as well as good food http://www.gitedetarsimoure.com/.

High ridges of the Diois hills

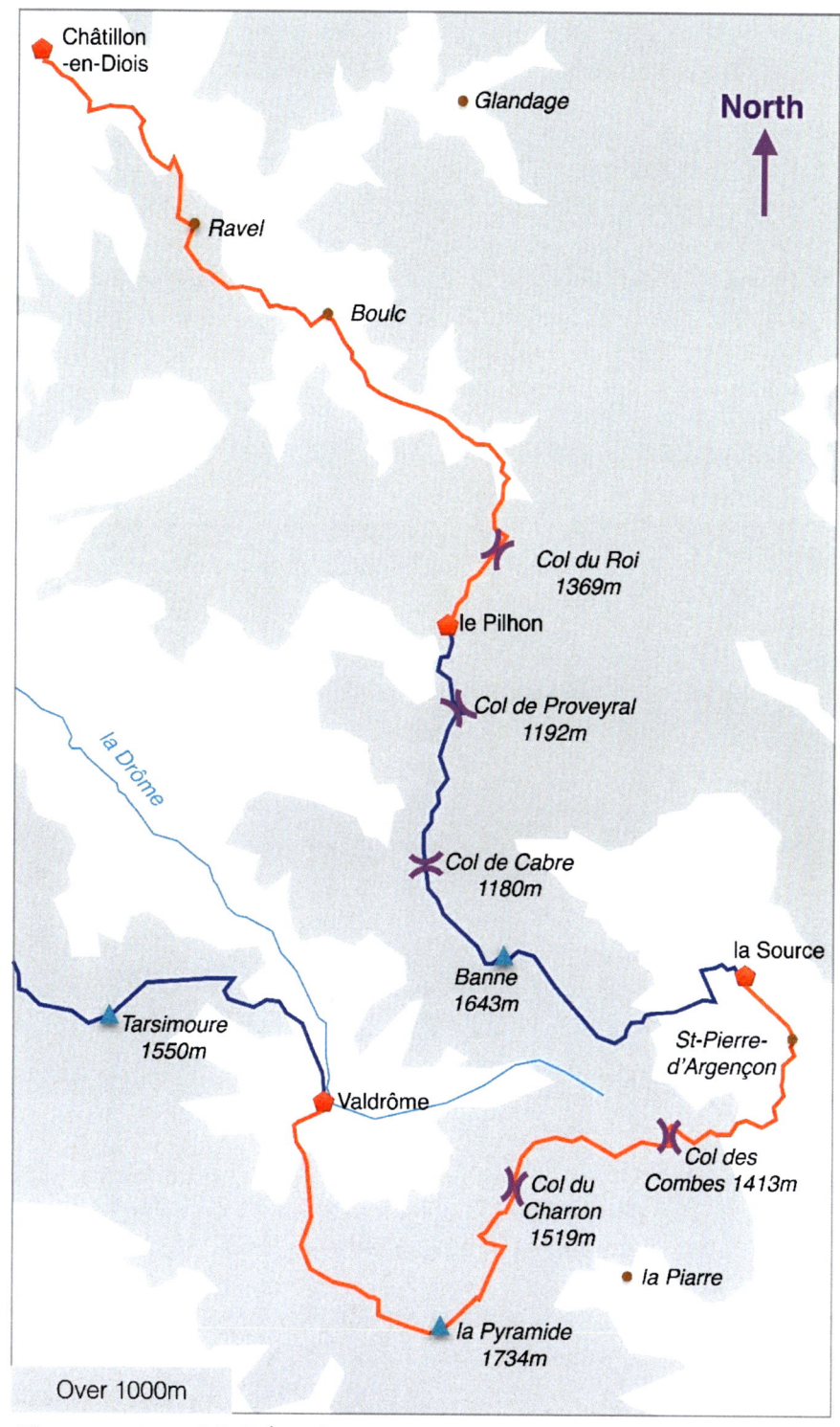

Eastern sections of the Diois Hills walk

Day 5: Valdrôme to Saint-Pierre-d'Argençon (785m)
22.8km, up 1,512m, down 1,529m, high point la Pyramide 1,735m, 8h50

This walk climbs to the summit of la Pyramide the highest point on this eight-day walk and continues along the northeast ridge of the Montagne de l'Aup. The ridge is more accessible than the previous day's traverse of the Tarsimoure, although limestone cliffs drop precipitously on its far side. The flowers at the beginning of June on the grassy north slopes of the ridge are, if anything, more spectacular than those seen on the previous day. After the traverse of the Montagne de l'Aup there is a descent of some 300m to a second ridge. This one is wooded and semi-circular, undulating for 3.5km to the pass between Valdrôme and Serres. By this stage it is early afternoon and the sharp 150m climb to the final ridge of the day is a taxing prelude to the long and poorly marked descent to St Pierre d'Argençon.

May flowers on the Montagne de l'Aup

Walking back down the road over the bridge the second turning on the right leads along the east side of Valdrôme. After half a km a path is followed to the left that heads southwards up a steep forested ridge. At 1,259m the path crosses a track and starts to traverse on the north-eastern flank of the Montagne de l'Aup, climbing gradually to the Cabane Pré Pourri. Then a path is followed that climbs gradually eastwards across lightly wooded hillside that is adorned with an amazing array of flowers in early summer (above). The path climbs onto open alp and then up to the col between the summits of le Duffre (1,757m) to the west and la Pyramide (1,734m) to the east. The route continues eastwards over la Pyramide and then descends 181m on steep grass to the Col de Lauzeto (below with the Pyramide rising behind). This col is a weakness in the ridge, where a path crosses and descends steeply to the hamlet of le Vissac. Our route continues eastwards along the ridge for another 2.2km, with views of the sharp limestone peaks of the Dévoluy in the background. It then heads steeply downhill to the west-northwest. At around 1,450m the path turns to the northeast and heads through forest to the Col du Charron.

The Pyramide from the Col de Lauzeto

The second ridge, le Serre du Charron, starts from this col. Despite being forested there are good views from the path. The start is easy enough, but there is a considerable amount of up and down before the road crossing at Col de Carabes is reached. Consequently, although the 150m climb up to the next ridge from this col may seem trivial, in baking sun this short sharp pull is quite taxing. It is indeed a relief to get to the shaded path that leads across a joining ridge to the Col des Combes.

There has been a reclassification of paths on the descent. Now, on reaching 1,069m, the trade route to the valley, the GRP: Tour du Buèch waymarked with red and yellow flashes, starts to traverse through the woods

Mountains of the Provençal Rim

north-north-westwards, but our route follows what used to be GR94 to the northeast. This heads more or less straight down the 4 km to St-Pierre-d'Argençon. It no longer has GR waymarks, but is shown as magenta dashes on the current IGN map. After passing through the village a walk north-westwards along the side of the railway for just over a km leads to the Chambres/Table d'Hautes la Source www.lasource-hautesalpes.com. This pleasant stopover is run by an English family.

Looking across to the Tarsimoure from the summit of the Banne

Day 6: Saint Pierre d'Argençon to le Pilhon (1086m)
16.8km, ascent 1,357m, descent 1,053m, high point Banne 1,643m, 6h10

The start of the walk turns right from la Source along the road. After passing through a double bend a left turn is taken onto a track that is followed south-westwards across the railway. Then, at a T junction our route turns left and continues south-eastwards for about 0.6km, where a left fork is followed, still to the southeast, across a brook. Some 0.25km after the fork a footpath is followed to the right that climbs up a pleasant ridge, which soon becomes wooded. At 1,079m, at a four-way junction of paths, the right hand option is taken to the northeast. This path reaches a track at 1,317m, which is followed uphill onto open alp at 1,479m. From there it is a stiff climb eastwards to the dome-shaped grassy summit of the Banne at 1,640m. This is a great view point of the impressive circle of mountains that surround Valdrôme and feed the headwaters of the River Drôme. It is possible to appreciate the profile of the Tarsimoure ridge, with its steep northern end, which was scrambled down two days earlier (above). From the summit of the Banne it is a pleasant westward descent to a forested ridge where the path follows the crest north-westwards to Col de Valdrôme. Then there is a descent on the right flank of the ridge, which leads to the main road between Die and Gap at the Col de Cabre (1,180m).

The route continues northwards from the col on the GR91 variant, which at first climbs gradually and then steeply to a col on the west ridge of the Chauranne. From there this pleasant undulating path continues in a generally northwards direction to the hamlet of le Pilhon and the excellent gîte d'étape le Pilhon www.gitelepilhon.fr/welcome.php?lang=eng. Nadia and Patrick Verleye are attentive hosts, who organised a party-type evening meal in the courtyard in front of the house when the author stayed there. They provided plenty to eat and drink and when two riders passed on horseback they too were treated to refreshments (below).

Party time at le Pilhon

Day 7: Le Pilhon to Châtillon-en-Diois (570m)
21.3km, up 1,060m, down 1,556m, high point Col du Roi 1,369m, 6h50

Take the track that runs in front of the church climbing north-eastwards from the village. When this reaches 1,282m follow a path to the left from the track that goes up to the Col de Roi. On the map this path is marked as a footpath with black dashes rather than in magenta of a public footpath. Nevertheless, it is an excellent route to the next valley, is used by mountain-bikers and is way-marked with the orange circles that signify an equestrian route. The path leads down through forest in zigzags to a dirt road through the hamlet of la Taravel, where there are some spectacular vertical limestone flakes. Soon the road becomes metaled and this is followed west-north-westwards down the quiet and pretty Bonneval to the village of Boulc. On reaching the village pump you may wish to drink from this refreshing source. After this the route turns left down the D174. The GR95 footpath is followed to the right, where this road crosses a bridge over a stream and turns left,. Initially this footpath heads northwest along the edge of fields, filled with poppy-red wheat in June 2014 (below).

Poppies in the wheat in the Bonneval

The GR then climbs to the west and later northwest on a somewhat tortuous route through forest, where careful attention has to be paid to the red and white way-marks. After reaching 1,046m the GR descends to the hamlet of les Ferriers, before continuing north on a lane to Ravel. In this second hamlet there is another refreshing fountain with delightfully cool, clear water. From there the route heads uphill to the west on a track that winds round to the north and then forks as it enters forest. Both paths lead to Châtillon en Diois. GR95 heads uphill to the left, but the pleasant well-made rocky path is followed to the right gradually descending through scrubby forest above a spectacular limestone gorge. At 1,025m the path levels off and rounds a spur to the left and then descends, again gradually, around the Combe Noire. Eventually the path comes out of this cirque and continues to descend to the west. On reaching a T junction with GR95 the route turns to the right and goes along the GR into Châtillon-en-Diois. Across the main street a lane is followed past a café up to the Gîte d'Étape de Chatillon http://www.gitesdechatillon.fr/pages/3.php. There is a warm welcome here, excellent food and comfortable bunk beds.

Day 8: Châtillon-en-Diois to Die (396m)
19.3, ascent 1,353m, descent 1,556m, high point Montagne de Label 1,173m, 7h00

The walk on the last day climbs to the Balcon de Glandase on GR95 and follows an up and down course on this footpath to Die. The GR runs north-westwards on the lane outside the gîte. After a little over half a km it leaves the lane to the left and climbs diagonally through woods, at first south-westwards and then to the west. After levelling off the path divides and the right fork is followed, zigzagging up the steep south face of the Montagne de Label and crossing its east ridge some 1,880ft above Châtillon. The path then traverses on the east side of the north ridge of the montagne (below), eventually crossing the ridge at the Col des Caux.

Traversing to the Col des Caux

The westwards descent on the GR loses 450m before reaching the jaws of a narrow pass where our route joins a broad dirt track that heads north without entering the pass. The track climbs to the Col de l'Abbaye from where GR95 descends to the Pas de la Roch, bypassing some of the loops in the track. At this pass there is shade by the side of a stream that is probably too murky to risk filling a water bottle. Again the route turns before the pass and climbs northwards on a path that runs along the edge a wood to the left of a field. On coming to a clearing the path joins another dirt track, which is followed to the left, going through long zigzags before reaching the Pas de Bret. From this pass it is all descent to the outskirts of Die. Eventually the path joins an unclassified lane that leads to the D742. A few meters to the left down this road is a very welcome drinking fountain outside a campsite. After a further 0.5km the road joins the main street through the old town. This is followed to the right through the centre of Die to la Petite Auberge lapetiteauberge.com, where the walk started eight days before. You may consider it time for a shower and then a glass or two of that cool sparkling Diois wine, but somehow, as can be seen below, beds claimed the author's two walking companions before they could indulge in such refreshments.

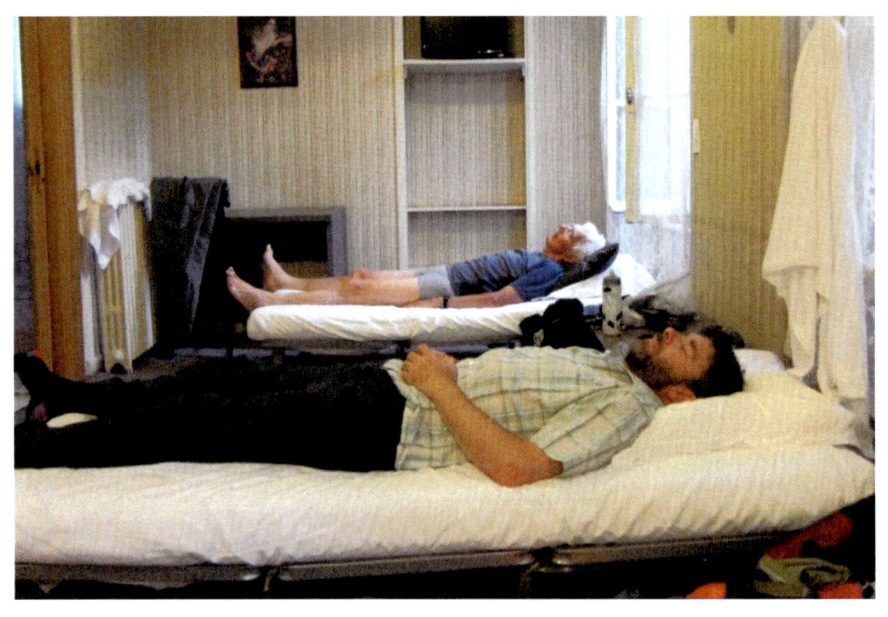

Casualties of the heat at the end of the last day's walk

5 CHAPTER
ESCARPMENTS OF THE DÉVOLUY AND VERCORS
A 9-day walk of 167km with 11,605m ascent from Lus-la-Croix-Haute to Grenoble

Few people in Britain seem to be aware of the Dévoluy. This is surprising as these hills form an impressive ring of sharp limestone peaks that reach more than twice the height of any mountain in the British Isles. The 65km long circumference ridge encircles a hidden green valley, of exquisite beauty.

The first two days of this tour make up a circular walk, starting from Lus-la-Croix-Haute, by the headwaters of the river Buëch. Initially a high rocky pass is crossed leading to a gîte d'étape in the pastures of the Dévoluy. The following day the return to Lus uses the other mountainous pass across the western Dévoluy escarpment.

The route then crosses the road between Grenoble and Sisteron and climbs into the Vercors where a complete south to north traverse of the 68km-long eastern escarpment is undertaken. The southern 25km of this escarpment consists of a chain of steep-sided hills, while the northern 42km takes the form of a sustained line of east-facing cliffs rising to a succession of jagged peaks. The western side of these peaks generally has a shorter, more gradual fall to the Vercors plateau. The high point and climax of the walk is the summit of the Grand Veymont (2,341m), which is also the highest point in the Vercors. Finally on the last day, after climbing the Moucherotte, the most northern peak of the chain, there is a descent of some 1,700m to Grenoble.

The western escarpment hills from the meadow above the Cabane du Chourum Clot Day 2

Summary of the route

Day 1, Lus-la-Croix-Haute (1,020m) to Lachaup in the Dévoluy (1,393m)
19.8km, up 1,389m, down 1,024m, high point Col des Aiguilles 2,009m, 6h50

Day 2, Lachaup to Lus-la-Croix Haute (1,020m)
21.6km, up 1,463m, down 1,833m, high point the Col de Charnier 2,103m, 7h46

Day 3, Lus-la-Croix-Haute to Glandage (858m)
17.1km, up 1,321m, down 1,491m, high point l'Aupillon 1,744m, 6h26

Day 4, Glandage to les Nonnières (864m)
20.9km, up 1,599m, down 1,615m, high point the Crête de Jiboui 1,723m, 7h00

Day 5, Les Nonnières to Richardière (1,039m)
17.3km, up 1,220m, down 1,046m, high point Pre de la Font 1,826m, 6h04

Day 6, Richardière to Gresse-en-Vercors (1,205m)
15.6km, up 1,484m, down 1,326m, high point Grand Veymont summit 2,341m, 6h19

Day 7, Gresse-en-Vercors to the Refuge de la Soldanelle (1,453m)
17.9km, up 1,351m, down 1,082m, high point Côte Vialin 1,606m, 6h25

Day 8, Refuge de la Soldanelle to the Auberge des Allières (1,426m)
14.7km, up 1,082m, down 1,106m, high point Col Vert 1,766m, 5h21

Day 9, Auberge des Allières to Grenoble (209m)
22.1km, up 696m, down 1,926m, high point le Moucherotte 1,901m, 6h38

Total distance 167km ascent 11,605m, average 18.6km, 1,289m ascent

A vulture flying through the Col des Aiguilles day 1

Escarpments of the Dévoluy and Vercors

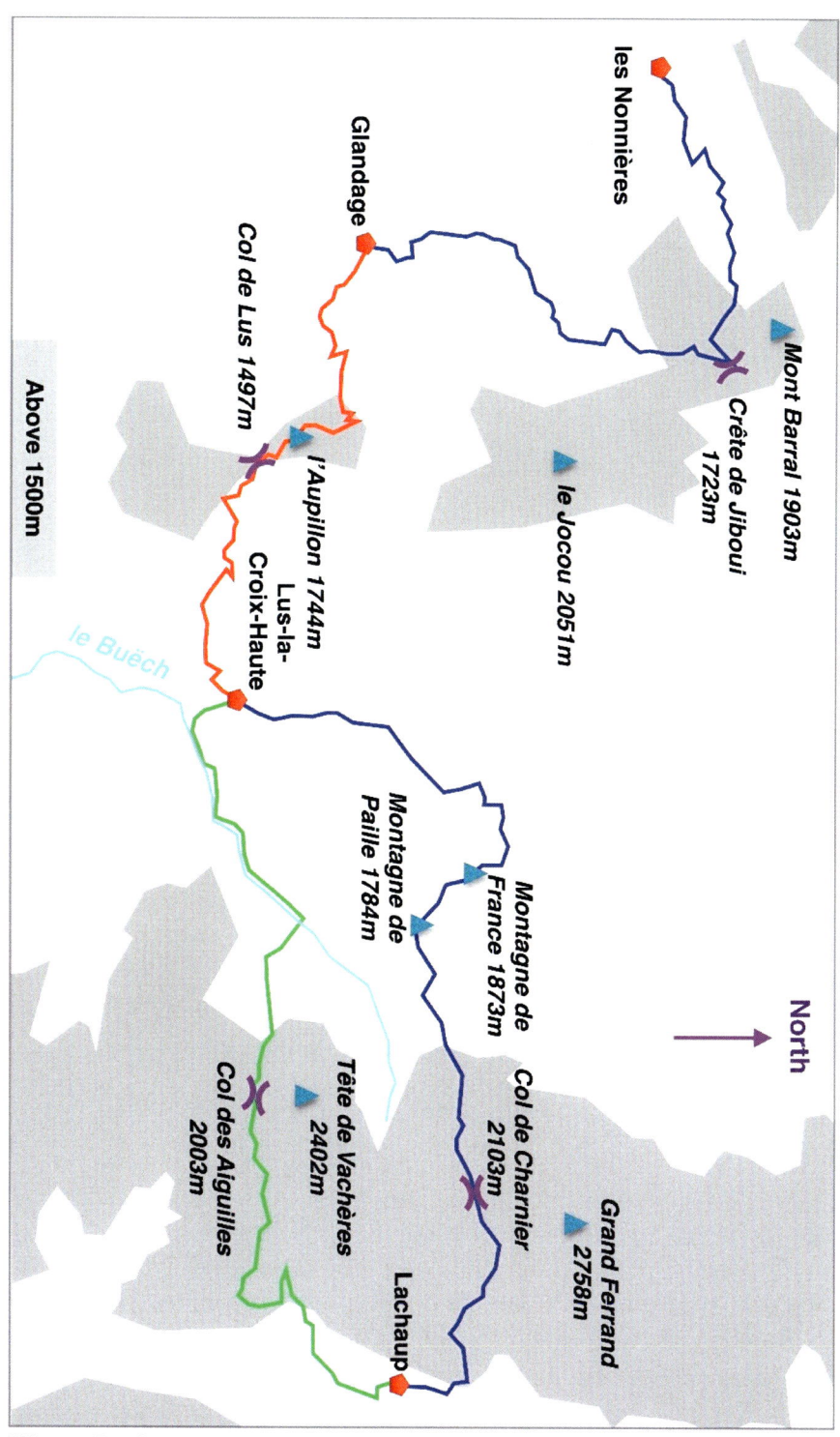

Western Dévoluy and Eastern Vercors first 4 days

Journey to Lus-la-Croix-Haute (1,020m)

From Lyon St Exupery Airport a hourly bus gets to Grenoble Gare Routier in about an hour and five minutes. Seats on the bus can be booked in advance, which is worthwhile as the service is often busy. Theoretically it should be possible to get a train from the adjacent Grenoble railway station to Lus-la-Croix-Haut. Unfortunately the author has had problems with this service with cancellations due to strikes and "operational difficulties". In this case a taxi for the 77km journey to Lus cost about 140€ in 2015. The train south from Lus runs to Gap where more regular trains go to Aix-en-Provence, Marseille and Vallance. The Hotel de Commerce in Lus http://www.hotel-commerce-lus.com. is an unpretentious, welcoming Hôtel with a lively bar/restaurant, frequented by the locals. It is a good place for walkers to stay.

The challenging way to the Dévoluy on the first day

Day 1, Lus-la-Croix-Haute to Lachaup (1,392m)
19.8km, up 1,389m, down 1,024m, high point Col des Aiguilles 2,036m, 6h50

GR94 heads southward from the main square, passing the Gîte d'Étape le Point-Vergule at the edge of the village. There is then a gentle climb through woods for about 0.6km before the path splits and the GR descends leftwards steeply to the mouth of the Gorges de Buëch. The route then follows the north bank of the river upstream, at first on a path and then a track that joins up with the D505. Rather than slavishly following the GR it is quicker to follow this pleasant lane through the opposed steep ridges that form the narrow entrance to the beautiful Jarjatte valley. The valley is encircled by the craggy limestone hills that will be explored during the next two days. Some 2.2km into the valley the road crosses the Buëch. After this a right turn leads into the village of la Jarjatte. The couloir that is going to be crossed and the surrounding pinnacles fill the view ahead (above). On the far side of the hamlet GR94 leaves the lane and heads south-eastwards on a grassy path that runs to the right of a ski lift. The path, marked with the usual red and white grande randonnée way-marks, soon becomes shaded by shrubby trees. It then joins a metaled road that leads to the start of a second ski lift where the GR leaves the road to the right following a switchback of a track that heads eastwards to the left of the second ski lift. On reaching a rough road the GR continues on the far side up a path that climbs steadily along a wooded ridge. As the path becomes steeper the woodland peters out in a huge cirque of rough limestone scree. In 2015 the author followed the way-marks up the ridge until he reached some small cairns that suggest the route crosses a deep, steep gully to the right. On the other hand the red and white way-marks continue straight ahead. A line of stones placed across the way-marked path correctly indicates this is now obsolete, for erosion has made it seriously unsafe to cross the gully higher up. Following the cairns, there is a delicate descent into the gully and up its far side (below).

The problematic gulley on the way to the Col des Aiguilles

On leaving the gully the route heads straight uphill on scree and patches of grass, initially in the absence of either a clear path or way-marks. Soon the way-marked path is joined once again. This then climbs in steep zigzags up the scree between the rock-faces of l'Haute Buffet to the right and the Tête Vachères to the left. The angle eases and the scree gives way to grass on the final approach to the Col des Aiguilles. At this point during our walk four huge vultures swept through the gap between the Aiguilles, circled round the Tête Vachères and then passed over the col again (photo page 98). These magnificent birds were not the only flying company. There were groups of alpine choughs, but also the continued, unwanted presence of swarms of buzzing flies.

From the col the prospects in all directions are magnificent. Looking back one can see in the distance the distinctive profile of les Trois Becs lying a full 50km to the west on the far side of Die. Ahead lies the enchanting green Vallon des Aiguilles. The snow-clad Écrin pyramid of the Vieux Chaillol can be seen through the Col du Noyer, a breach in the eastern Dévoluy escarpment.

The route round the barrier in the Vallon des Aiguilles

There is a comparatively short descent eastwards on scree to the grassy floor of the Vallon des Aiguilles. Then the path gradually works its way over to the northern edge of the valley until it comes to a bank beyond which the valley ends abruptly and there is a precipitous drop to a lower valley. The path turns right in front of the bank and crosses the valley stream before climbing to sloping rocks on the south side of the precipice (above). The red dots shown on the map indicate this is a delicate section of path, but these marks should only deter walkers who suffer from serious vertigo. The path is exposed but quite safe if care is taken. Once past the entrance to the hanging valley the path descends on easier, grassy ground passing to the left of a shepherd's hut. Some way beyond and below this hut the path divides. The GR continues to descend eastwards to the Col du Festre, but our route turns left above a fence and follows a grassy path between short pines and larches. In this section of the walk the author noted several clusters of browny-yellow-capped Slippery Jack (Suillus Bovinus) mushrooms projecting through the grass. These, as the name implies, have a slimy cap, but if one removes the skin from the cap and the spongy gills these mushrooms can form the basis of a delicious soup.

Wild roses on the way to Lachaup.

The path gradually winds round into the valley below the limestone cliff at the mouth of the Vallon des Aiguilles. In late spring, when there is still much snow on the hills, a substantial waterfall cascades over this cliff, but in summer the valley stream retreats underground and its exposed bed below the cliff is dry. The path continues to climb to 1,526m where it becomes obscured in the rich hay meadows that surround a shepherd's hut, the Cabane de la Rama. Beyond the hut, on the far side of the stream-bed a grassy track winds down the valley, eventually joining the white limestone-chip lane that runs northwards from the Col du Festre. This lane is followed to the left giving fine views of the Dévoluy pastures and the impressive cliffs of the surrounding hills. Wild roses abound on the verges (above). Where the lane forks, the left branch leads into the hamlet of Lachaup. The Gîte d'Étape le Rocher Ronde http://gitesdudevoluy.free.fr/gite/Le_Rocher_Rond.html lies on the far side of the hamlet to the right of the road. This well-run friendly gîte has good bunk rooms, hot showers and inside toilets.

Day 2, Lachaup to Lus-la-Croix-Haute (1,020m)
21.6km, up 1,463m, down 1,833m, high point the Col de Charnier 2,103m, 7h46

This outstanding walk, returns to Lus through the Col de Charnier, the other high walkable breach across the western escarpment of the Dévoluy. The start is to the north from Lachaup on a white limestone-chip lane that climbs gradually. After 1.1km a cairn marks a somewhat overgrown track that leads off to the left. This track heads westwards and then curves round to the right, climbing to a broad east-west ridge, where the track joins GR93. This goes westwards up the ridge in partial shade, shortcutting a winding track. Eventually the GR joins the track where it curves round another shepherd's hut – the Cabane du Chourum-Clot.

The way to the Vallon Charnier

To the south of the cabane the route leaves the track and climbs on a grassy path to a magnificent large alpine meadow. Rising on the far side of the meadow are the cliffs of the Roche Courbe. To the left of the Roche is a steep scree-filled valley, but the route goes up the Vallon Charnier on the right (above). After walking northwest across the meadow a point is reached looking down into the Vallon Charnier. The path then zigzags down to the floor of this green valley before climbing westwards below massive cliffs to the Col de Charnier, the high point of the day. This remote vantage point is surrounded by peaks. To the north are the screes below the cliffs of the Grand Ferrand, which at 2,758m is the second highest peak in the Dévoluy. Ahead and to the right lie the cliffs of the Tête du Lauzon, while at their base is a lofty green hanging valley with the little lac du Lauzon in its floor. Looking back down the valley the snow-capped Écrin peaks can be seen above the line of the eastern escarpment of the Dévoluy.

The descent from the Col de Charnier

The way down from the col follows a steep rocky path (above) that leads to the floor of the hanging valley, where it divides. The right fork, which has been somewhat eroded by livestock, runs above and to the right of the Lac du Lauzon. This path climbs steadily to the western lip of the hanging valley at 2,016m. From this lofty rim one can see ahead to the ridge that will be walked in the afternoon. The immediate task is to descend a steep zigzagging path that leads down the Pre de Ferrand. The gravel on this path has sections with ball-bearing-like pebbles that need to be treated with respect. When the path reaches the west ridge of the Tête du Lauzon it zigzags down the line of the ridge before crossing a floral meadow on the right. At the bottom of the meadow the path runs along the edge of a cliff and then passes a scrubby beech wood before crossing another meadow to the Col de Croix. It is possible to escape from here to the valley of the Buëch and then walk back past la Jarjatte to Lus. This would cut about an hour and a half off the day's long walk, but in fine weather in early summer it would be a tragedy to miss the wonderful ridge walk that lies ahead, with its exceptional array of alpine flowers.

The floral way forward from the Col de Croix

The route continues on GR93 climbing west-south-westwards from the col. Initially this follows the line of the ridge, although there is neither an obvious path, nor any way-marks for the first 1.2km from the col. The left side of the ridge soon becomes a cliff, while floral meadows fall away to the right. The first 100m or so of steep ascent heads for a wooden cross on the ridge climbing through an amazing meadow (above). St Bernard lilies and common spotted orchids were everywhere among the mass of other flowers at the end of June 2015. After the cross the angle eases somewhat and the route temporarily leaves the ridge heading for a low limestone band that stretches northwards from the ridge. This band is climbed without difficulty to a limestone platform. From there a short grassy descent leads to a shallow col. There red and white way-marks start, although there is still no obvious path. The climb continues up the ridge to the rocky summit of the Montagne de Paille

Escarpments of the Dévoluy and Vercors

(1,729m) which is a great viewpoint for the western escarpment hills. The cliffs of this summit impressively overhang the Jarjatte valley (below, looking back to the Col de Charnier and the morning's descent).

The overhanging-summit rocks of the Montagne de Paille

The ridge next heads north-westwards and descends a little before rising to a high point at 1,859m. Here the ridge splits. Ignore a fork to the left rising south-westwards to the summit of the Pointe Feuillette (barrel) and take the right fork that continues north-westwards still on GR93. At last there is a distinct path that goes first to the right and later the left of the wire fence that marks the crest of this sharp, but grassy, ridge. To the right, there are fine views of the western Dévoluy escarpment (below). Eventually the path descends northwards to the Col de Jargène, where it turns westwards and goes down a mainly grassy valley.

Looking back to the Grand Ferrand from GR93 on the Montagne de France

Before reaching woodland at the bottom of the valley GR93 turns left and follows the grassy left bank the stream that flows down the edge of the wood. At the confluence with another stream the original stream is crossed to a white stony track, which is followed south-westwards, through a gorge, to the hamlet of les Amayères. Here the route turns left onto a lane and continues southwards, in the shade of a tall box hedge. Where the road curves round to the right the GR continues straight on, following a stony track that climbs a little before reaching a crest. From there Lus-la-Croix-Haut comes into view across the fertile valley. It is then a matter of following the red and white way-marks of GR93 on stony tracks and paths through the meadows and fields to Lus, the Hôtel de Commerce and much-needed liquid refreshment.

Escarpments of the Dévoluy and Vercors

Day 3, Lus-la-Croix-Haute to Glandage (858m)
17.1km, up 1,321m, down 1,491m, high point l'Aupillon 1,744m, 6h26

Today the walk crosses from the Dévoluy to the Vercors. On clear mornings, looking east from the square outside the hotel, the aiguilles crossed on the first day are silhouetted against the low sun (below). From the far corner of the square the route heads south-westwards on the D754 road and soon turns left onto a lane signposted to the hamlet of Le Cheylard.

The Col des Aiguilles, silhouetted in the dawn light, seen from Lus-la-Croix-Haute

At the end of the lane GR94 is joined, which leads off to the right on a wide grassy path between two houses. It continues on the edge of a hay-field climbing into woodland. Where the path forks, GR94 falls steeply to the right through the wood to a footbridge over l'Unel stream, a northern tributary of the Buëch. Beyond is the main Grenoble - Sisteron road. Diagonally to the right across the road the route turns into a lane that passes under the railway line on its way to the hamlet of la Caire. The lane curves round to the south and immediately before a stream a right turn onto a stony track leads up the floor of the Gorges de Toussière. The track climbs steadily, with the torrent on the left running noisily at the base of a shallow mossy gorge. Limestone cliffs rise to the right. Eventually the track crosses the torrent and soon afterwards winds round to the south coming to open ground. After another 0.2 km the track comes down to and crosses the stream. Here the route leaves GR94 and follows a track that runs just west of north and then generally north-westwards along the edge of a wood with a field falling to the right. Soon it passes the ruined Templiers' chapel, which was being restored in 2015 and then climbs, still to the northwest, up scrubby open ground for about 0.5km. The path onward to the Col de Lus is not always clear and careful navigation is required.

On entering steep woodland the path starts to traverse, curving gently to the right and crossing the stream that runs down the apex of the valley. After a further 0.21km, at a junction of paths, a sharp turn is made to the left and the path, now labelled le Chemin des Templiers, climbs west-south-westwards, soon reaching the stream crossed on the lower path. The path follows the stream bed for a few meters before coming out onto open meadow, first climbing south-south-westwards and then gradually winding to the northwest. After passing between two woods and crossing a further meadow the path reaches the Col Navite (1,399m) and a junction of four paths. Our route continues on le Chemin des Templiers traversing westwards through woods. Gradually the path narrows and the fall to the right steepens. At one point the path descends to a rocky gully with a stream and there is a short scramble up rocks on the far side. Then the path, which in places becomes a forest track, climbs gently north and then north-westwards to the Col de Lus.

The Western Dévoluy Escarpment from the Col des Prêtres; arrows mark the passes crossed

From the col there is a steep climb northwards and then north-westwards up a broad open ridge to the summit of l'Aupillon. The delectable ridge along the summit, at times broadens to support a tiny plateau of lush grass. In one place the path temporarily descends to the right below difficulties and just before the end of the ridge drops steeply to the right down a grassy slope and then starts to traverse northwards. Now one can look back and see the white rock face of the ridge just crossed. The path then descends to the Col des Prêtres. The photo above is taken from the floral meadows at this col looking across to the western Dévoluy escarpment. The right arrow indicates the Col des Aiguilles crossed on the first day, while the left arrow shows Col de Charnier, the highest point on the second day. From the Col des Prêtres the route heads north-westwards across the face of the Serre les Têtes and after 0.35km follows a signed path to the left that descends the steep hillside in several long shallow zigzags. Eventually the zigzags end and the path is crossed by a wire fence. The route continues round the cirque below the Col des Prêtres. There is no longer a visible path but yellow and green way-marks on pine trees help route-finding through the scrubby meadow. On the far side of the cirque the way-marks lead into woods where a forest track descends steadily on the south side of the valley. After 1km this track joins a larger stony track, coming up from the right and the route continues westwards to a fault in a sharp limestone ridge. This fault is another Col des Aiguilles.

The track from Maillefauds to Glandas

On the far side the route descends steeply on a narrow stony track that runs just east of south. Eventually the track turns to the northwest. At the second bend a way-marked path is followed to the right that descends more gently through pine woods. On coming to a meadow the route skirts above this to the right and then descends along a line of scrub to the top of the hamlet of les Maillefauds. Here a track running past the upper walls of the houses heads north-westwards. This pleasant and partially-shaded way (above) leaves the hamlet and follows a traversing course between fields, ending at the Village of Glandage. At the main road in Glandage a left turn leads, after about 0.2km, to the Château le Colombier, which lies a short way up the first side road to the left. This delightful small chateau lecolombier.diois@gmail.com offers elegant accommodation and an excellent table d'hôte. On arrival a message on the door asks customers to phone the owner 04 75 21 21 51, who may be out of range of a knock on the door.

Day 4, Glandage to Hotel Mt Barral at les Nonnières (868m)
20.9km, up 1,599m, down 1,615m, high point Crête de Jiboui 1,723m, 7h00

The day starts returning up the main road through Glandage. About 0.8km past the village the road bends round to the northeast and our route follows the metaled lane that doubles back to the left. A footpath sign at the corner indicates the Grande Traversée du Vercors in the direction of les Sucettes de Borne. The footpath starts as a grassy track running from the right of the lane between the houses of the hamlet of la Revolt. Then this becomes a fiercely steep path that heads upwards through the woods in short oblique zigzags. Fortunately the path soon becomes civilised and starts to climb gently in long zigzags, making for an easy and shaded ascent of the steep wooded hillside. After gaining nearly 300m a col is reached and the route continues northwards on a pleasingly shaded broad path that climbs gently across the west-facing wooded hillside. Some 1.75km from the col, when the path has risen to 1,265m, it meets a track. Here the route heads to the right uphill and after a few paces turns left at a crossing of tracks.

Les Sucettes de Borne

This new track also traverses northwards for a while before descending gently to the east-northeast. After veering left at a fork the route continues to descend in the same general direction. Now there are glimpses to the left of impressive vertical limestone flakes known as les Sucettes de Borne (above).

Gradually the track makes its way to the base of the valley, where the stream is crossed by stepping stones. On the far side a right turn onto a white limestone-chip lane leads up the valley. At the apex of a hairpin bend the route continues straight ahead, to the right of the stream, on a narrow, but well-made, track. This track climbs northwards for a while at a shallow angle before winding up more steeply to the Refuge la Tour de Berg. After going through a couple of bends on the track a path is followed that short-cuts further bends before rejoining the track just before the refuge. This building is set on meadowland above the woods of the valley. From there the track continues north-eastwards. After a further 0.7km another track is crossed and the route continues on a broad path signposted to the Col de Jiboui. This path heads steadily uphill through mainly coniferous woodland, at first north-north-eastwards and then to the north. After about 0.7km the rim of a steep cirque is reached and this is followed to the col.

The summit of Mt Barral with Grand Ferrand in the background

To the east of the col a fine floral alp rises to the Crête du Jiboui, which joins the 2,051m Jocou in the south with Mont Barral in the north. A climb to the low point of the crête (1,723m) is rewarded with magnificent views along the crête and eastwards to the Dévoluy and Écrins. If you are feeling energetic, make the short sharp climb up the south ridge of Mont Barral to its limestone summit at 1,905m (shown above, with the Dévoluy in the background). It is possible to continue down the far side of Mt Barral to the Col de Menée, (this is described in reverse on day 2 Chapter 1). As the descent from this col on the road to reach les Nonnières is rather long, retracing ones steps to the low point of the Crête du Jiboui and descending on GR93 to les Nonnières is probably the more pleasant option. The detour to the top of Mont Barral and back takes a little under an hour.

The descent from the Crête du Jiboui on GR93 starts on a grassy track that makes long zigzags across alpine meadow in a generally westerly direction. As is indicated on the map this passes well north of the two shepherds' huts that lie below the Col de Jiboui. On reaching a stony track the GR turns right along this and after 0.25km descends left from the track to a path by a stream. This way-marked path follows the line of the stream for a short distance before climbing on the far side of a rapidly-developing gorge. As the path enters woodland it joins a forest track that descends to open meadows surrounding the ruined Ferm du Désert. Here a left turn crosses a small stream before continuing through the long grass westwards to another wood. There the GR follows a track that descends steeply on the left side of a gorge before joining a white gravel lane. Turning right onto this lane the route continues more or less horizontally across a stream and then along the north side of the valley.

Looking down through the trees from GR 93 to les Nonnières

Eventually the lane joins the D120 road, which connects the Col de Menée with les Nonnières. The GR shortcuts the next downward loop in the road and rejoins the road for 0.3km before leaving to the left and traversing southwards on a narrow path across a steep cirque. The picture above shows a glimpse from this path of les Nonnières far below in the valley, almost hidden by the trees. The higher unobscured village is Bénevise. After the path winds round to the left it doubles back descending westwards above a stream, eventually joining a well-made stone track. This track is followed for a while before the GR leaves the track for a path heading down to the left, which in turn joins a lane that goes into les Nonnières. On reaching the main road a right turn leads, after a few yards, to the Hotel le Mont Barral: www.hotelmontbarral-vercors.com. This has comfortable rooms and a good restaurant.

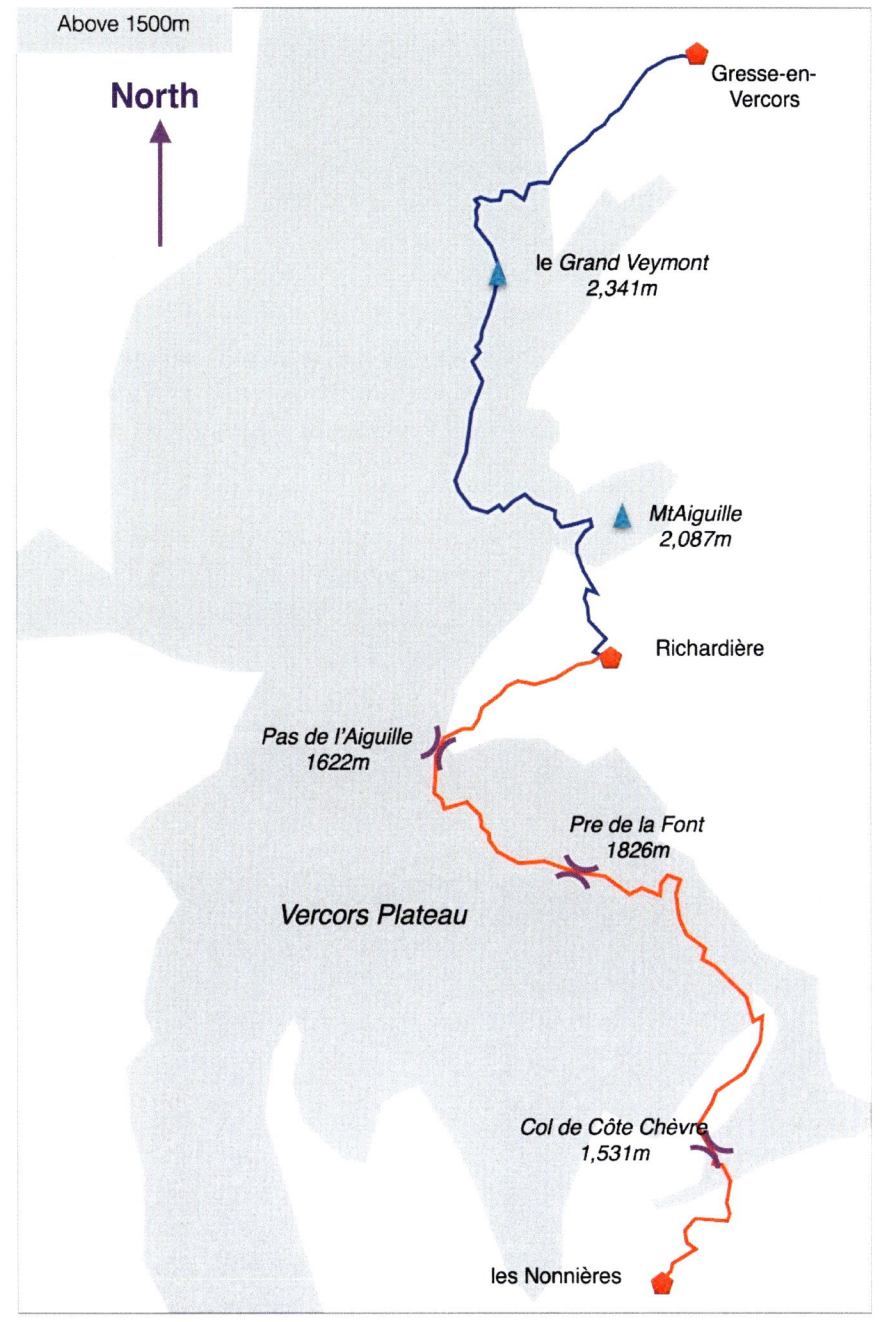

Dévoluy Vercors Walk days 5 and 6

Day 5, les Nonnière to Richardière (1,039m)
17.3km, up 1,220m, down 1,046m, high point Pre de la Font 1,826m, 6h04

This walk crosses the ridge east of the Rocher de Combau, the tall knife-like rock that rises to the north behind les Nonniére. It then descends to the high Vallée de Combau before climbing to the main plateau of the Vercors.

A few metres up the lane that runs east from the hotel a local path, signed to the Col de Côte Chèvre, is followed to the left. This climbs diagonally eastwards up the steep hillside. Eventually the path reaches a level area with fields. After going along the edge of the first field the path turns left at a wire fence, crosses the meadows and then curves round to the right as it climbs to the Col-de-Menée-road. On the far side of the road a well-made, shaded path starts to climb just west of north, but soon winds round to the east. After passing to the left of a wooden shack it continues climbing to a forested plateau.

Looking down to the Rocher de Combau from the Col de Côte Chèvre

On reaching a meadow hidden in the forest the way-marks indicate a right turn passing in front of the ruins of a stone house. The path marked on the IGN map goes straight ahead at this turning, but the distances of the two routes to the Col de Côte Chèvre are similar. After the ruins the way-marked path heads northwards through the meadow. At the far end of the open ground this route continues through scrubby forest climbing gradually to the Col de Côte Chèvre. From there one can look down on the Rocher de Combau (above). On the far side of the col the well-made path descends diagonally, losing 175m before reaching the lane running up the Vallée de Combau. A right turn onto the lane passes the Gîte Auberge du Combau and continues for 1.8km, to a car park.

A broad well-made stony track heads west from the car park. This goes through one hairpin bend before climbing northwards and then northwestwards on the west side of the valley. Where the track reaches a large cowshed the route continues on a well-trodden path. Initially this heads north-eastwards, but soon turns to the northwest, climbing steadily to the Caban de l'Essaure, where the path splits. The most direct route is to take the left fork that continues north-eastwards up the valley to the Col du Greuson. Alternatively the right fork heads north to the col that leads to Chichilianne. From this col a clear path traverses in a generally westerly direction to the Col de Greuson. The latter route has the advantage of giving fine views to the east of the Écrins and Dévoluy. From the head of the Col de Greuson the path continues to climb in a meandering fashion between the limestone outcrops and hollows of the Vercors plateau. Care needs to be taken to keep to the route, for the wandering nature of the path and the complexity of the landscape can easily lead one astray. After reaching the high point, Pre de la Font, at 1,826m the route descends through a dense growth of nettles and docs that surround the Bergerie de Chamoussel. This green and stinging flora characterises areas where stock have been confined around bergeries and vacheries throughout the Alps. Fortunately normal flora returns after a short distance.

The Grand Veymont and Mont Aiguille from below the Bergerie de Chamoussel

Next the path gradually works its way round to the northwest and then after climbing a little comes to a col with bare limestone gravel and a stunning view of Mont Aiguille and the Grand Veymont to the north (above). As can be seen the striking rock tower of Mont Aiguille has a flat grassy summit that is cut off from access on all sides by sheer cliffs.

The descent from this viewpoint is north-westwards through green pasture with widely-spaced mature conifers. The path makes one long zigzag before reaching the octagonal small wooden Cabane de Chaumailloux, which is also passed on the first day of the walk from Die to Briançon (Chapter 2). From the cabane the route heads north across grassland, passing to the left of a dew pond and then the graves of 8 members of the French Resistance, who were killed near here towards the end of the Second World War.

The steep descent from the Pas d'Aiguille

The path starts to steepen after the graves, as it enters the Pas d'Aiguille and makes its way in short zigzags down the north side of the gully (above), eventually leading to the fields to the west of Richardière. This path is reasonably wide, but it is steep and exposed in places. These factors, combined with the loose scree, mean that caution should to be exercised on the upper part of the descent. Eventually the gradient eases and the path widens as it enters forest. At the bottom of the gully the path passes a memorial to the French Resistance and then joins a limestone gravel track that winds through unshaded fields for some 2km to the hamlet of Richardière. Here is the Hotel au Gai Soleil de Mont Aiguille www.hotelgaisoleil.com, with its shaded terrace; another good stopover for walkers.

Day 6, Richardière to Gresse en Vercors (1,205m)
15.6km, up 1,484m, down 1,326m, high point Grand Veymont 2,341m, 6h19

This walk is a highlight of the tour. First climbing to the Col de l'Aupet, which forms the western shoulder of Mont Aiguille, the route then crosses onto the Vercors plateau before making a complete traverse of the Grand Veymont. From the summit of this highest peak in the Vercors there are unrivalled views northwards of the Eastern Escarpment of the Vercors (below).

The Vercors Eastern Escarpment stretching northwards from the Grand Veymont

The way to the Col de l'Aupet backtracks along the lane of arrival the previous evening. Where two lanes join from the right the route follows a track that runs between these lanes and is signed to the Col de l'Aupet. After one bend a path to the left short-cuts to a higher track. This track is followed north-eastwards and then to the northwest. After about 0.5km a signpost indicates a path to the right to the Col de l'Aupet. This well-made path is way-marked with yellow flashes. It zigzags up though forest for some 2km before emerging into a steep limestone-scree cirque and continuing to zigzag up to the col.

The path heads west from the Col de l'Aupert descending for a short distance out of the trees to more open ground. It then traverses left around the cirque of the Montagne de l'Aupert for 0.7km, before zigzagging south-westwards up scree to reach the Vercors Plateau, at the rather indistinct Pas de la Selle. Here the path divides and the right fork is taken. This curves round to the north to the Pas des Bachassons. From there the path past the Cabane des Aiguillettes and over the Grand Veymont is now shown on the IGN map as an unclassified route drawn with black dashes. The reason for this declassification is unclear for the route is quite straightforward and was enjoyed by the author's 13 year old granddaughter in August 2016 (below). From the Cabane des Aiguillettes there is 500m of sustained ascent, initially zigzagging up scree, then passing a series of false summits before reaching the true summit.

The south ridge of the Grand Veymont with Mt Aiguille in the background

From the top, the steep hillside that falls away to the right on the way up the ridge, is replaced by near vertical cliff. Looking back there is a stunning view of Mont Aiguille, seen above with the tops of western Dévoluy escarpment poking through the clouds in the distance. The path deviates a little way from the cliff-edge on the descent to the north and is relatively straightforward, with a bit of a scramble down the last section into the Pas de la Ville. From this pass there is a good, but steep path that zigzags eastwards down to the car park at the base of the ski lifts. It is another 2km on the road from the car park to the village of Gresse-en-Vercors and the Auberge Buissonnière www.buissonniere.fr/ which lies to the south up the main street.

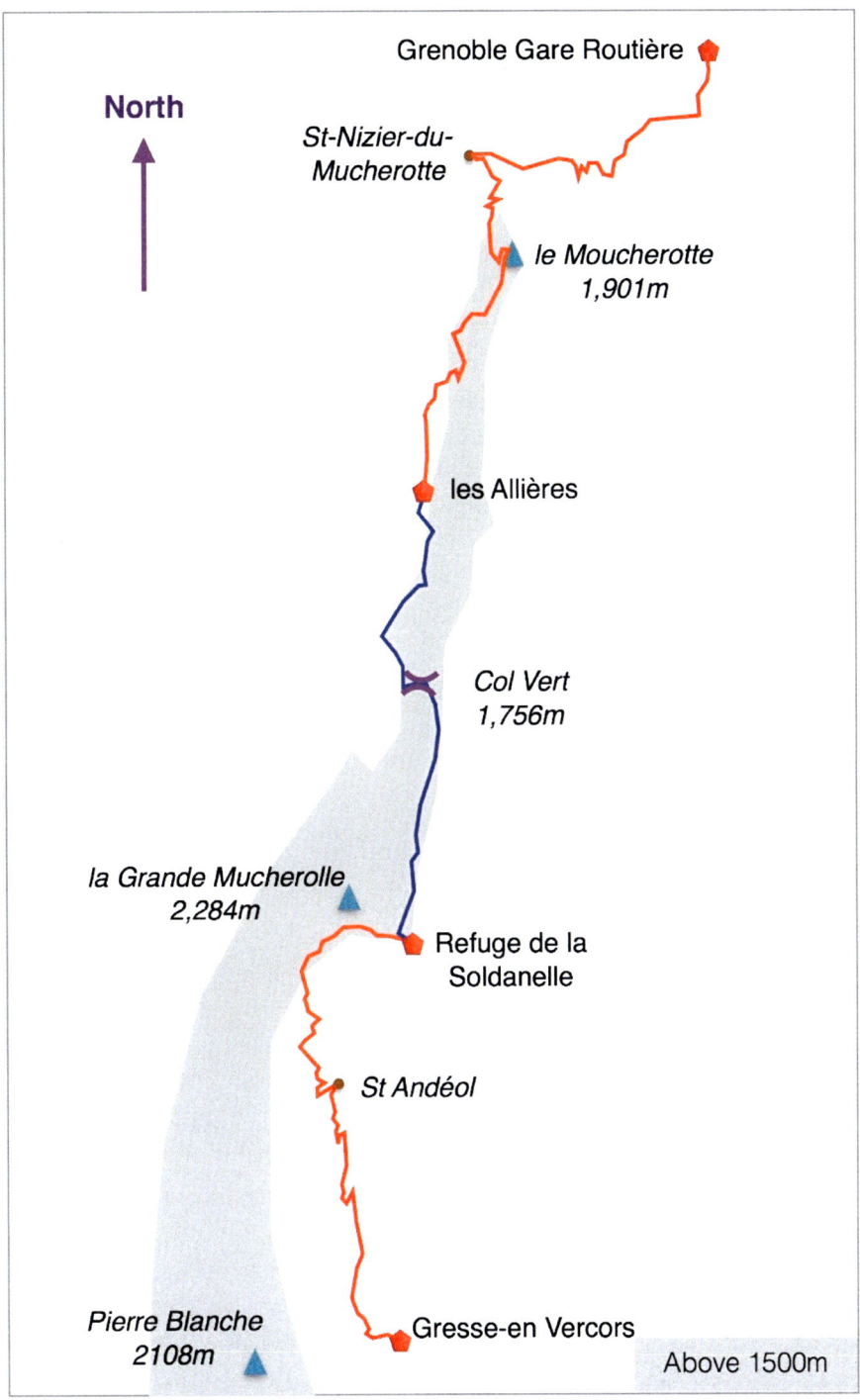

The Dévoluy Vercors Walk days 7 to 9

Day 7, Gresse en Vercors to Refuge de la Soldanelle (1,453m)
17.9km, up 1,351m, down 1,082m, high point Côte Vialin 1,606m, 6h25

This walk climbs to the spectacular Balcony Path on the Eastern Escarpment of the Vercors and ends at a refuge, sited dramatically below the cliffs of les Deux Sœurs.

Going north down the main road from the hotel the route turns left onto the road that passes in front of the church and then heads downhill. As the road flattens off, a track to the right leads steeply up to a lane that runs west-north-westwards along the top of a broad ridge. There is a fine view from this lane to the cliffs of the Grand Veymont (below). After continuing straight ahead at the next crossroads, the lane later forks and the route turns right onto a farm drive. This drive winds round to the north, but before reaching the farm buildings a track is followed to the left that descends to the hamlet of les Grands Deux.

The cliffs of the Grand Veymont from the northeast

On the far side of the hamlet a left turn onto the D242 leads to the sister hamlet of les Petits Deux, where the road turns to the north and climbs gently towards the Col des Deux. A few metres past the col a track is followed to the right that traverses on the steep wooded eastern side of the Berrrièves valley. From this track there are fine views of the cliffs of the eastern Vercors escarpment rising on the opposite side of this valley. Some 1.6km further north the route leaves the track for a shaded path to the left that gradually descends through a long zigzag to the Berrrièves stream. Counterintuitively, the path then heads south along the bank until it reaches a footbridge. On the far bank a track northwards joins a lane that winds up to the D242 road in the southern outskirts of the village of St Andeol. Here a lane that runs below the main road is followed into the village. At the end of the lane steps to the left lead up to the main road in the centre of the village. On the far side of this road follow a lane that winds round to the west. After the last house the lane becomes a track that curls to the south. It then goes through a hairpin bend and heads north into woodland. This track climbs to about 1,150m before traversing in a generally northern direction for some 3km. Where the track bends to the right and just before the Ruisseau des Combes, a yellow and green way-marked path is followed to the left that climbs in increasingly steep zigzags up the escarpment.

The Eastern Balcony path with the Deux Sœurs in the background

The last section of this path comes out onto steep floral alp before reaching the Eastern Balcon path (above). The route now traverses north-eastwards on the light-reflecting, limestone-scree. Occasionally it passes through the top of the forest giving welcome shade. Gradually the escarpment and path wind round to the east. The terrain now becomes quite steep and there is some exposure as the path traverses under the Grande Sœur Agatha. Later, when the path starts to wind once more to the north, the going become easier. At the apex of this bend a good path leads steeply down a ridge to the Refuge "la Soldanelle":

www.lasoldanelle.com/. This is an excellent hut, not least for its spectacular location (below). The bunk room is under the terrace and there is a hot shower and indoor flush toilet. The evening meal served to the author on the terrace was memorable for the superb pasta bake with wild garlic and trompette de la mort mushrooms (*canterellus cornucopoides*).

The last rays of the setting sun on Mt Aiguille seen from the Refuge Soldanelle

Day 8, Refuge de la Soldanelle to Auberge des Allières (1426m)
14.7km, up 1,082m, down 1,106m, high point Col Vert 1,766m, 5h21

After climbing back the 150m to the foot of les Deux Sœurs, the route continues north along Balcon Est des Vercors. Most of the 7.7km on the northern section of the Balcon path to the Col Vert is relatively easy going. It is only the last km to the col that has a modest ascent of 250m, but again this is on a well-made path. The descent on the far side of the col is on a steep, zigzagging, stony path that joins up with GR91 at the Roybon Bergerie. The route turns right (northeast) onto this GR, traversing at about 1500m through the forest on the western side of the escarpment. The path is well made and

Escarpments of the Dévoluy and Vercors

shaded, making the first 2.5km delightfully easy-going. After this the path comes out onto steep open hillside, with some sections rounding rocky outcrops spectacularly, but perfectly safely (below). Eventually GR91 again enters woodland and descends steadily to the Collet du Furon, where it comes to rough pasture. On the far side of this col the path joins a track. Where this track divides the stopover for the night, the Auberge des Allières www.aubergedesallieres.com/ can be seen lying between the two branches of the track a short way below the col. The auberge is a deservedly popular place to visit as it serves excellent food and is only a modest walk up a track from the car park on the road that runs from Lans-en-Vercors to the local ski station.

GR91 on the way to Auberge des Allières

Day 9 Auberge des Allières to Grenoble Gare Routière (209m)
22.1km, up 696m, down 1,926m, High Point le Moucherotte 1,901m, 6h38

The last day's route continues along GR91 on the west side of the eastern Vercors escarpment. Although the Moucherotte is 1,901m, it is still a relaxing walk getting there, for the start is from 1,426m and the well-made tracks rise at a steady gentle gradient. Also much of the ascent, if done in the early morning, is in shade.

Walking northwards along the track above the auberge leads, after a little more than a km, to the parking area of the Serre ski station. The GR crosses the base of this car park and then descends briefly to the D1061 road just before the base of the ski lifts. The red and white flashes indicate the way across the bottom of the ski station and onward on a broad track that winds up to the summit of le Mucherotte. If clear, there are fine views from here down to Grenoble and on to the Écrins, as well as back south along the Eastern Vercors Escarpment.

The GR starts the descent heading west-northwest before turning south-south-westwards on a track (below). A path is followed from the track that zigzags down to the northwest and then north. After this the route becomes quite complex and there are several diverging paths to confuse, but the GR waymarks should keep the walker on the right course down to the village of St-Nizier-du-Moucherotte. From there the author followed GR9 down to Grenoble, which is pleasant enough, but there is much to be said for taking a bus from St Nizier Village to Grenoble Gare Routière http://mhd.ens.fr/GdR/horaires-bus.pdf, especially in a heat wave. From the morning cool at the summit of the Moucherotte it was 40ºC when the author reached this city at the junctions of the rivers Drac and Isère.

The start of the descent from the Mucherotte looking back along the Eastern Escarpment

6 CHAPTER
CRÊTES AND BAISSES OF THE ALPES MARITIMES
A 6 day circular walk from Saint-Martin-Vésubie of 109km, with 9,447m ascent

In September 2002, when the author did this walk the Rhône Valley had flooded the previous week and many of the vineyards were unable to salvage sufficient quality grapes to make domain wines that year. Those steep hills of les Alpes Maritime that lie west and south of the French Italian border were able to spill this deluge into the Tinnée, Véssubie and Roya rivers and remained walkable. The rains at the end of August also brought an abundance of fungi including prized culinary specimens such as ceps and girols.

The first day of this six-day circular walk clears the cobwebs from the lungs as it climbs a ridge north-eastwards from St Martin Vésubie at 962m to a high point of 2,496m. This is followed by a descent to the Relais des Merveilles for the night. The following day there are two big climbs. The first crosses the Pas de l'Aupette (2,511m) to the Vallon des Merveilles and from there the second climb goes over the Baisse[1] de Vallauretta (2,379m) before descending to an auberge in the hamlet of Casterino. For the next three days the route mostly follows GR52 westwards through serious mountain scenery to St Dalmas where the land drains into the river Tinée. The final day again climbs to a high ridge and follows this south-eastwards on GR5 before descending to the Vesubie valley and back to St Martin.

The first 2 weeks in September are a good time to tackle this walk as the high passes are clear of snow and the huts are still open. The baisses crossed on days 3 and 4 of this walk would have been snow climbs in second half of June

---

[1]Baisse is a synonym for col or pass, used in the Alpes d'Haute Provence and Alpes Maritime.

2008 when the author did the walk from Menton to Briançon described in Chapter 7. On that occasion it was necessary to bypass these sections, taking a more southerly route from the Vallon des Merveilles to la Madone de Fenestre.

The way forward from the 2,691m Baisse du Basto on day 3

Crêtes and Baisses of the Alpes Maritime

Day 1: St-Martin-Vésubie (962m) to Relais des Merveilles (1,579m)
18.8km up 2,093m, down 1,466m, high point Cime de la Vallette de Prals 2,496m, 8h00

Day 2: Relais des Merveilles to Casterino (1,543m)
20.1km, up 1,708m, down 1,736m, high point Pas de l'Arpette 2,511, 7h49

Day 3: Casterino to Refuge Nice (2,232m)
15.7km, up 1,452m, down 808m, high point Baisse du Basto 2,691m, 6h00

Day 4: Refuge Nice to le Boréon (1,502m)
15.2km, up 1,165m, down 1,867m, high point Pas du Mt Colomb 2,548m, 5h59

Day 5: le Boréon to St-Dalmas (1,290m)
20.4km, up 1,423m, down 1,631m, high point Col du Barn 2,453m, 7h20

Day 6: St-Dalmas to St-Martin-Vésubie (962m)
18.8km, up 1,606m, down 1,937m, high point on Mt Tournairet 2,036m, 7h22

Total 109km, 9,447m ascent; daily average 18.2km with 1,575m ascent

A chamois and her kid at the base of the Caire de la Madone on day 4

Mountains of the Provençal Rim

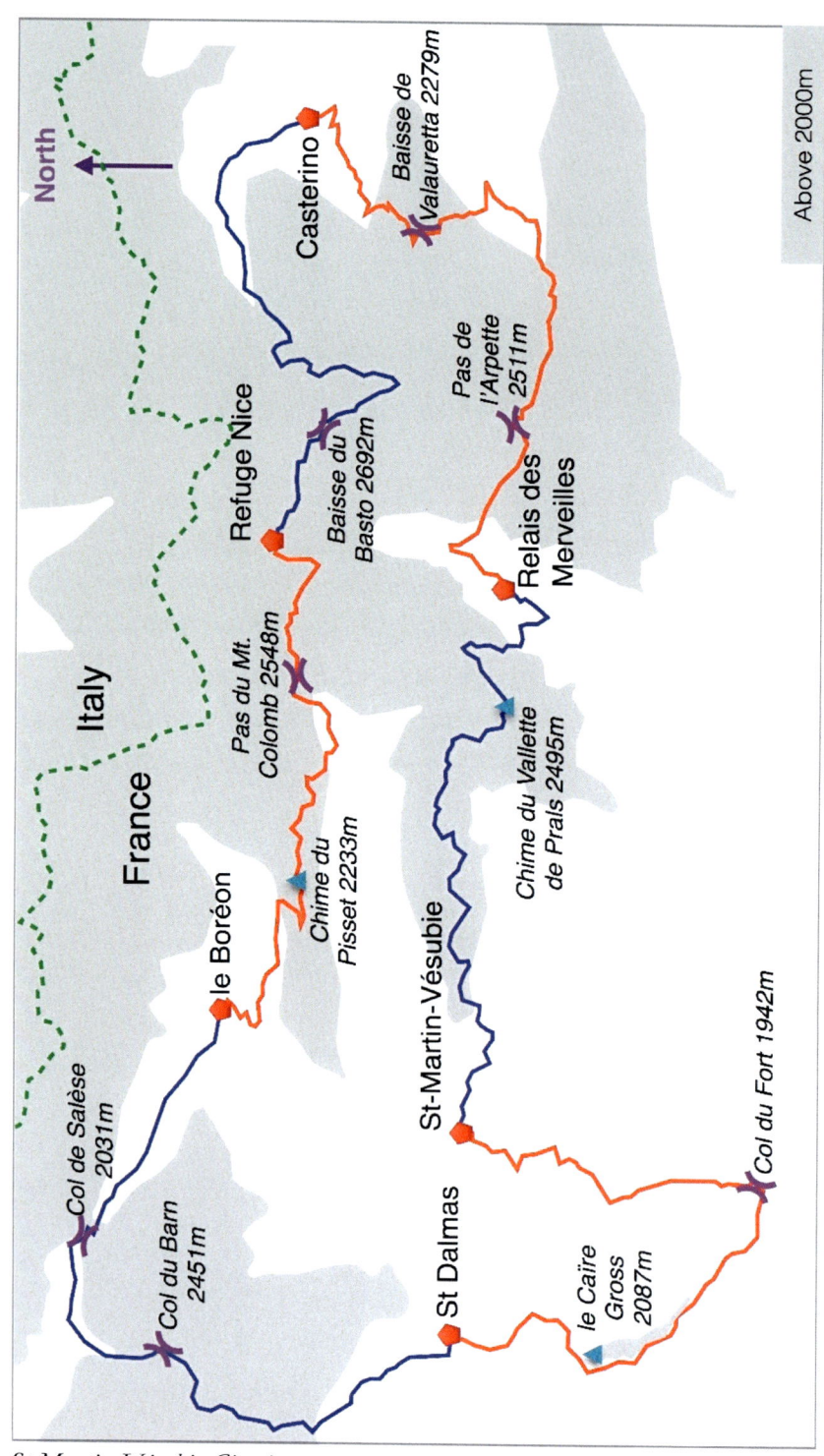

St-Martin-Vésubie Circuit

130

Getting to St Martin-Vésubie (962m)

The 730 line bus http://www.alpha-loup.com/pdf/bus.pdf is a convenient and inexpensive way to get to St Martin. This leaves from Terminal 1 at Nice Airport. The bus stops in the centre of St Martin, where there are several options for accommodation.

Day 1: St-Martin-Vésubie to le Relais des Merveilles (1,579m)
18.8km, up 2,093m, down 1,466m, high point Cime de la Valette de Prals 2,496m, 8h00

There is an energetic and unrelenting climb eastwards from St-Martin-Vésubie up steep forested hillside to the Cime de la Palu. This climb of 1,144m, covered in 2.5km, is followed by an airy 8km ridge walk (below) reaching a high point at the Cime de la Valette de Prals.

Approaching the Tête de la Lave where the ridge curves to the south

The main road in the centre of St Martin goes through a hairpin bend and the walk starts along the short lane that runs southeast from the apex of this bend. A left turn at the end of the lane and then the second right joins the road carrying GR52a. This is followed eastwards and after it curls round to the south a path is taken to the left at signpost [337]. Signposts in the Alpes Maritime helpfully carry numbers, which also appear on the IGN 1:25k maps. These signpost numbers are written within square brackets in the text of the next two chapters. The path from [337] climbs steeply eastwards through forest to [342], where a left turn soon crosses a route forestière. This forest track is met once again at [343] where, on the far side of the track, the righthand of two paths is followed climbing eastwards. After taking the left fork at [344] the path carries on climbing through forest. Eventually it comes out onto open hillside just below and to the right of the summit of the Cime de la Palu (2,132m). The path then joins the grassy east ridge of the cime and the route follows a right fork at [348], where there is a cross. The traverse along the ridge continues mainly on its southern side, but occasionally goes along the crest itself.

The Relais des Merveilles

After passing several summits the path reaches the Baisse de Férisson and signpost [297], where the route continues straight on. At [298] on the Tête de la Lave the ridge curls round to the south. The path sticks to the right of the crest of the ridge before climbing to the high point of the day – the summit of the Cime de la Vallette de Prals. From this summit the route descends northeast to the Baisse de Prals. A little further along the ridge, at signpost [365], the route forks to the right and circles round to the south before descending steeply in zigzags. Eventually this path reaches the D171 valley road at the hamlet of St-Grat. A left turn up the valley leads to the Gîte d'Étape le Relais des Merveilles (above), a pleasant overnight stop www.relaisdesmerveilles.com. This gîte d'étape should not to be confused with the CAF Refuge de Merveilles, a stopover on the Menton to Briançon walk (Chapter 7), which is passed on the following day's walk.

Day 2: le Relais des Merveilles to Casterino (1,543m)
20.1km, up 1,708m, down 1,736m, high point Pas de l'Arpette 2511, 7h49

The second day is also strenuous, this time crossing two high passes. From the Relais de Merveilles the walk climbs to the Pas de l'Arpette before descending past the Refuge des Merveilles, into the Vallon de la Minière. It then climbs northwards through the Baisse de Vallauretta (2279m) to the Vallon de Fontanalba and down to the hamlet of Casterino.

The start continues up the valley road to its end at the Pont du Countet. On the far side of the bridge a path, starting from the information boards, heads south-eastwards up the Vallon d'Empuonrame. After zigzagging up the headwall of the green and partially-wooded lower valley the path continues to climb the upper hanging valley through the tree line, to the Pas de l'Arpette. The descent from this col starts north-north-eastwards and then winds round to the east-southeast, continuing in this direction past the south side of the Lac Long Superior to the CAF Refuge de Merveilles (below).

Lac Long Superior with the CAF Refuge de Merveilles to the right of the dam

Beyond the dam the path leads down, between the Lac Long Inferior and the Lac Saorgine to the wooded floor of the Vallon de la Minière, forking left at signposts [90], [89] and [89a]. There is another fork at a bridge over the valley stream. The left branch is followed across the bridge, which then continues to signpost [383]. There the route turns sharply to the west and stays going in that direction for about 0.5km. It then turns north-westwards and climbs some 760m to the Baisse de Vallauretta. From this col the path heads westwards to the foot of a cliff, where it joins the path running north-eastwards down the Valon de Fontanalba. After passing the Refuge Fontanalba a right turn is taken at [390], that continues down a track to the D91 road at the southern edge of the hamlet of Casterino. A left turn up the road leads to the popular Auberge Val Casterino http://www.valcasterino.fr/.

The beautiful Valmasque valley in autumn sunshine

Day 3: Casterino to Refuge Nice (2,232m)
15.7km, up 1,452m, down 808m, high point Baisse du Basto 2,691m, 6.00

The walk sets off north-north-eastwards up the lane from the auberge. After a couple of km a left turn is taken at signpost [394] onto the path up the Valmasque Valley. This valley is lightly wooded with larches and in September 2002 there was an abundance of larch boletus (slippery jacks) in the surrounding grass. The path runs alongside the valley stream with its multiple waterfalls, a delightful place in warm autumn sunshine (above). Some 5km from the road the valley path starts to zigzag up the headwall below the CAF Refuge de Valmasque. This is set at the north end of a spectacular hanging valley in which three large lakes have been scraped out of the granite floor by ancient glacial action. Behind the lakes to the west lies a succession of high rocky peaks that end at Mont Clappier (3034m) on the international border ridge. A left fork at signpost [98] leads to [97] and a view looking down to le Lac Vert and the Refuge de Valmasque (below). Another left turn at [97] passes le Lac Noir and then le Lac du Bastuo Some way beyond the south end of the third lake right turns are taken at signpost [96] and then at [95], where GR52 is joined. This is followed north-eastwards up granite boulders to the high point of the day, the Baisse du Basto (photo page 128).

Lac Vert and the Refuge de Valmasque

The footpath on the far side of the col descends steeply on scree and is marked on the IGN map with dots, suggesting a delicate route. In snow-free conditions, with care, there should be no difficulty getting to the valley floor. The mountain scenery here is remote and awe-inspiring. The path passes a series of tarns as it makes its way down the valley towards the Refuge de Nice. This is situated on a rocky ledge overlooking the Lac de la Fous. On-line booking for this CAF refuge is available http://refugedenice.ffcam.fr.

Day 4: Refuge Nice to le Boréon (1,502m)
15.1km, up 1,165m, down 1,867m, high point Pas du Mt Colomb 2,548m, 5h59

GR52 continues from the Refuge de Nice descending to the lac de la Fous and passing along its western shore. A short way below the dam at signpost [416] the GR heads uphill to the right climbing steeply to the Pas du Mt Colomb (seen below from the Madone de Fenestre side). This is an excellent and enjoyable route. Although marked as being delicate on the IGN map, in snow-free conditions, it should not present serious difficulties.

The steep descent from the Pas du Mt Colomb

There is a shorter steep descent on the far side, which with care is also straightforward. On the other hand, after the angle of descent eases, much of the way down to the Madone de Fenestre is across tiring boulder fields that do not make for relaxed walking, or rapid progress. The Madone de Fenestre is a cluster of buildings based on the site of a 12th Century Benedictine Monastery. The ancient chapel is well worth a visit. The buildings on the north side of the courtyard house the Madone de Fenestre CAF refuge, which was a favourite stop on the walk between Menton and Briançon, described in Chapter 7.

The current walk continues past this pleasant refuge to le Boréon. The path onwards starts from signpost [356] at the west end of the Madone de Fenestre car park and climbs in zigzags north-westwards and then continues to ascend round the hillside to the west. At [429] the upper path to the right is taken. Eventually it reaches the broad grassy ridge that separates the valleys of le Boréon and la Madone de Fenestre. After passing over the Cime du Pisset the ridge descends to the Pas des Roubines de la Maïris. There a path leads off to the right at [431]. This descends northwards entering forest. At signpost [432] a left turn leads onto a path that traverses through the forest and continues to [383]. The view below looks to the frontier hills from near this signpost. A right turn at [383] leads downhill to the D89 road in le Boréon, which at this point crosses a bridge on the way to the Col de Salèse. Some 0.3km past the bridge a turning on the right leads, after a few yards, to the Gîte du Boréon, http://giteduboreon.monsite-orange.fr, which is on the right side of the road.

The border hills in late June seen on the descent to le Boréon

Day 5: le Boréon to St-Dalmas (1,290m)
20.4km, up 1,423m, down 1,631m, high point Col du Barn 2,453m, 7h20

The walk follows GR52, which runs past the Gîte du Boréon. At the bottom of the lane this continues westwards along the D87. After 1.7km, at signpost [399], the GR descends on a path from the left side of the road through the forest to a wooden bridge across the Boréon Torrent. On the far bank the route follows the footpath to the right, upstream climbing gently through the woods. After about a km the path crosses the stream over another bridge before passing a bend in the road and continuing westwards below the road, only rejoining this at the hairpin bend immediately before the Col de Salèse. On the far side of the col the road has a white gravel surface and the GR bypasses its first two loops. It then keeps to the road for 1.5km before following the red and white GR waymarks along a track to the left past a vacherie. Just before these cow sheds the GR veers off the track to the left, climbing through forest into the Valon de Barn. After crossing the valley stream on a wooden bridge the forest gives way to delightful lightly-wooded pasture. The path eventually starts to climb the screes at the head of the valley that lead to the Col du Barn, from where there are fine views back to the border hills (below).

The border hills in September from the Col du Barn

Lac Gros lies on the far side of the Col du Barn at the bottom of a rocky cirque. The path winds round the right side of this cirque before crossing the bar and descending into a second hanging valley. This has a much greener floor, surrounding the four Lacs des Millefonts. The path passes to the left of these lakes and works its way to the ridge running down the south side of this valley. On reaching the Col de Veillos on this ridge GR52 heads south towards a mountain road, which is crossed. The path now runs below the road for a while, but when the road starts to loop southwards the path crosses to its east side and then heads southwards down a partially wooded valley that leads to the village of St-Dalmas, where GR52 terminates. There is a gîte d'étape in the centre of the village http://www.gite-marmottes.fr, but the author chose to stay in a comfortable, but affordable small hotel, the Auberge des Mures http://www.aubergedesmures.com/fr. This is located on the right, a short way up the main road running northeast from the village.

Day 6: St Dalmas to la St-Martin-Vésubie (962m)
18.8km, up 1,606m, down 1,937m, high point on Mt Tournairet 2,036m, 7h22

The return to St-Martin-Vésubie involves another fine ridge walk. This heads south from St-Dalmas on GR5. At signpost [95] the GR heads southeast climbing up the wooded left side of a broad ridge. After crossing the ridge the path winds to the right round the head of a wooded cirque eventually reaching the Col du Voraire (1,710m). This lies northeast of the summit cone of le Caïre Gros (2,087m).

Looking back along GR5 past le Pertus to Mont Chalancha

The GR continues across the wooded northwest face of this hill to the Col des Deux Caïres, which lies on the west ridge of the le Caïre Gros. From there the path contours at about 1,950m on the steep west and then southwest side the long ridge running south and then southeast from the le Caïre Gros. The picture above looks back along GR5, showing a point where the path reaches a dip in the ridge at le Pertus, with the cone of Mont Chalancha in the background. After the Baisse de la Combe the ridge becomes more rounded and the path follows its thinly-wooded top. Where the ridge starts to rise to the summit of Mont Tournairet the path turns onto the north-western face and continues to the Collet des Trous. After passing on the south side of the next hill the GR reaches a track at the apex of a bend at signpost [320]. Here a left fork is taken onto a track away from GR5. Almost immediately at [321] a path marked in magenta dashes on the IGN 1:25k map is taken to the left. This path heads north across the Col du Fort and then descends steeply in zigzags to the Vacherie de Murans. A left fork is taken below the vacherie as the path follows the left bank of a stream heading just east of north. The path crosses a route forestière at 1,423m and on reaching another track at [322] crosses the stream and follows the right bank past [43]. The stream winds to the right and then at [44] the path crosses a bridge over the stream and climbs to a lane at [45]. The lane is followed to the right and at [46] a path is taken to the left that climbs into the village of Venanson, the upper left-hand village in the picture below, St-Martin-Vésubie lies in the valley on the right. From Venanson the road heading north is followed down towards St-Martin-Vésubie, taking the shortcuts, marked on the IGN 1:25k map, between loops in the road.

The route passes through Venanson, the hill village to the left, before descending to St-Martin

7 CHAPTER
TRAVERSE OF THE BORDER ALPS FROM THE SEA
A 15 day walk of 263km, with 22,619m ascent from Menton to Briançon

This walk is the first phase of an 82 day Grand Traverse of the Alps completed by the author between 2008 and 2013. The traverse started at Menton on the Côte d'Azure and after walking through the French and Swiss Alps and Dolomites finally descended to Vitorio-Veneto on the Adriatic coastal plain 1,500 km later[1]. The route described here, walked in late June 2008 ends in Briançon. It only occasionally follows GR5, the standard long distance path that heads north from Nice to Lake Geneva. Rather it takes a higher, more remote and challenging course, staying near to the French/Italian border.

This walk starts from Menton-Garvan harbour, just 1km from the frontier and in the first three days follows GR52 northwards. In keeping with the ascent profile of the whole walk the 1000m contour is first reached a little over 3km from the sea. After descending to Sospel the next two days' walks follow further ridges northwards over the Authion and then through the snow line to the Pas de Diable on the way to the Refuge des Merveilles.

On the fourth and fifth days the route, like the French-Italian border, turns to the west. Exceptional snow cover in June 2008 made it necessary to deviate to the south of GR52 on these sections of the walk, but this detour is an excellent walk in its own right. The continuation of GR52 from the Vallon des Merveilles to le Boréon, in the snow-free conditions of September 2002, is described in Chapter 6. On the 6th day the route briefly rejoins GR52 at le Boréon, but after the next col abandons grande randonnées and climbs northwest to the border and the ski resort of Isola 2000. The way forward then

---

[1] Walking the Alps from Mediterranean to Adriatic Ian CM MacLennan. The account of this walk here is completely rewritten and has different illustrations

becomes challenging but magnificent, climbing to the frontier ridge and following this for most of the seventh day, before making a vertiginous descent through the Pas de Beuf (below) on the way to the Italian Refugio Laus. From there the border is crossed again, before descending to the commune of St-Étienne-de-Tinée. This is followed by a long steep climb to les Lacs de Vens and the magnificently-sited refuge of the same name. The route then takes an unmarked trackless line along the border for several kilometres before joining GR5 to cross the pas de la Cavale and descend to the village of Larch.

Next the walk crosses the remote Chambeyron Alps, reaching the high point of the whole trek, before descending to the hill village of Fouillouse. The route then crosses the Upper Ubaye Valley and climbs into the Eastern Queyras. The night is spent at the Refuge de Basse Rua, before making an exciting traverse across the Pic d'Escreins to Ceillac. Once again the route joins GR5 for the final two days. This goes past the Château Queyras and into the Isoard Valley, before finally crossing the northern Queyras rim through the Col des Ayes and descending to Briançon.

Edging down the delicate, exposed descent from the Pas de Bœuf at the end of day 7

Stages on the route from Menton to Briançon

Day 1: Menton Garvan (sea level) to Sospel (409m)
18.3 km, up 1,820m, down 1,411m, High point the Colla Bassa 1,110m, 7h30

Day 2: Sospel to the Baisse de Camp d'Argent (1,753m)
21.5 km, up 2,423m, down 1,100m, high point Mont Giagiabella 1,902 8h45

Day 3: the Baisse de Camp d'Argent to the Refuge des Merveilles (2,115m)
12.8km, up 1,237m, down 850m, high point the Pas du Diable 2,432m 5h00

Day 4: Refuge des Merveilles to la Madone de Fenestre (1,903m)
16km, up 1,450m, down 1,678m high point Pas de l'Arpette 2,511m 6h30

Day 5: la Madone de Fenestre to le Boréon (1,530m)
13.4km, up 1,070m, down 1,474m, high point Cime du Piagu 2,338, 5h15

Day 6: le Boréon to Isola 2000 (2,050m)
20.2km, up 1,644m, down 1,112m, high point the Tête Mercière 2,491m, 7h15

Day 7: Isola 2000 to Rifugio del Laus (1,913m)
20.8km, up 1,884m, down 1,900 m, high point Tete Rougnous 2,694m, 8h30

Day 8: Rifugio del Laus to St-Étienne-de-Tinée (1,145m)
17km, up 776m, down 1,637m, high point Pas de Colle Longue 2,533m, 5h00

Day 9: St-Étienne-de-Tinée to the Refuge de Vens (2,366m)
10.8km, up 1,814m, down 607m, high point Crête des Babarottes 2,509m, 5h30

Day 10: Refuge de Vens to Larche (1,666m)
22.6km, up 1,175m, down 1,849m high point Pas de Morgon 2,714m 7h30

Day 11: Larche to Fouillouse (1,872m)
18.4km, up 1,639m, down 1,444m, high point Pas de la Couletta 2,774m, 7h15

Day 12: Fouillouse to the Refuge de Basse Rua (1,760m)
15.8km, up 1,342m, down 1,454m, high point Col de Serenne 2,674, 6h15

Day 13: Refuge de Basse Rua to Ceillac (1,636m)
15.8km, up 1,778m, down 1,890m, high point Pic d'Escreins 2,734m, 7h00m

Day 14: Ceillac to la Chalp d'Arvieux (1,675m)
20.1km, up 1,589m, down 1,622m, high point Col des Fromage 2,301m, 7h30

Day 15: la Chalp d'Arvieux to Briançon Gare (1,203m)
19.1km, up 978m, down 1,440m, high point Col des Ayes 2,477m, 6h15

Total 262.6km, 22,619m ascent, daily average 17.5km, 1,508m ascent

Mountains of the Provençal Rim

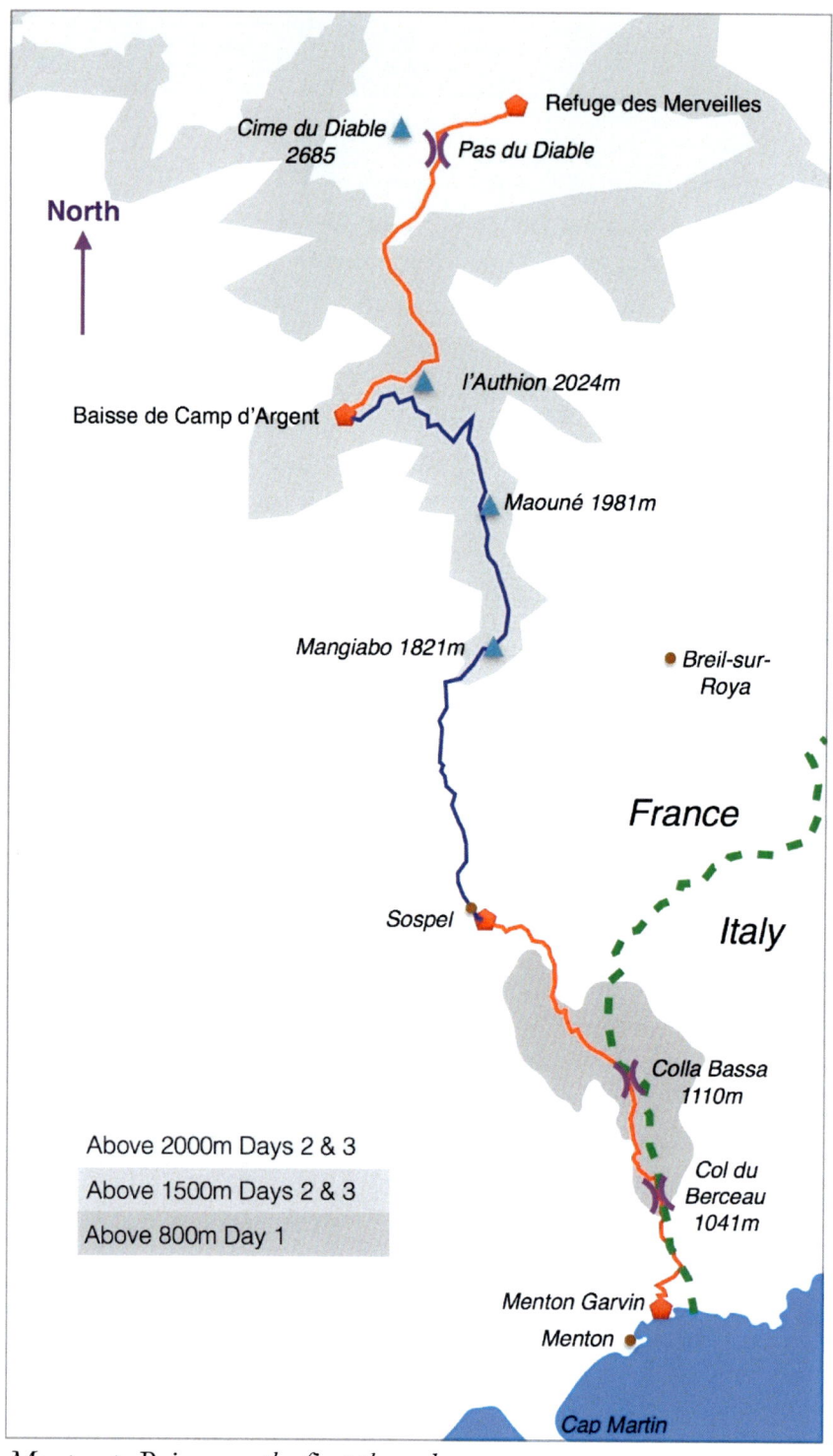

Menton to Briançon, the first three days

Day 1: Menton Garvan (sea level) to Sospel (409m)
18.3 km, up 1,820m, down 1,411m, High point the Colla Bassa 1,110m, 7h30

GR52 starts from the yacht harbour just east of Menton Garvan railway station, walking up Avenue Katherine Mansfield from the promenade and passing under the railway bridge. From there the red and white GR flashes lead up a narrow steep alley to the left, the Raccourci des Colombières, which starts between the garages of two houses. High walls flank the first part of the route providing welcome shade as it passes up successive passageways and across five terraced roads. The GR then passes under an elevated section of the autoroute, which protects the coastal towns from through traffic. After this the buildings peter out and Monte Carlo becomes visible to the west as the path climbs steeply in zigzags up delightfully fragrant herb-filled and floral hillside. Seven hundred meters above the sea there is a short respite in the climb, as the path crosses a relatively flat meadow, the Plan de Lyon.

From the Col du Berceau looking back to the start of the walk 1,092m below

To the right at the far side of the plan two limestone buttresses rise to the first high pass, the Col du Berceau. The path winds back and forth across steep coarse limestone scree in the gully between these buttresses. This path leads to the picturesque, pine-shaded grassy col (above), a great place to rest, after climbing 1,100m in 3.5 horizontal km from Garvan harbour. The foreshortened view down to Menton almost gives the impression that it would be possible to toss pebbles into the sea from this col. From the east side of the col it is only 0.15 km to the Italian boarder, but the GR stays in France, descending northwards across thinly-wooded hillside, losing some 300 metres before reaching a ruined castelet. After passing to the northeast of the ruins the route heads northwards, climbing gradually on a stony track to a second col, the Colla Bassa. From there a largely horizontal path traverses to the third pass, the Col de Razet. As mentioned in Chapter 6 the signposts in the Alpes Maritime are numbered and these are helpfully shown on the IGN 1:25k maps. The post at the Col de Razet is numbered [90]. From there a gentle 5km descent, mainly through woods, leads to the ancient town of Sospel. At the mid-point of the descent there is a slight rise to a clearing in the woods, where there is a stone water trough. Soon after this, at signpost [107], the path veers to the northwest and descends to a broad track that leads to the metaled D2566 road at a hairpin bend.

One day is over and refreshment is taken on the terrace overlooking Sospel

Instead of following GR52 down the road to Sospel, the route heads uphill in the direction of the Col de Chastillon. This leads to the Auberge Provençal www.aubergeprovencale.fr/ which lies at the apex of the second hairpin bend, marked [106] on the map. This comfortable two-star Logis Hotel has a good restaurant and a scenic terrace overlooking the ancient town of Sospel (above).

Day 2: Sospel to Baisse de Camp d'Argent (1,753m)
21.5 km, up 2,423m, down 1,100m, high point Mont Giagiabella 1,902, 8h45

There is a lot of climbing on this walk, but it is not technically difficult and quite manageable in a day. It is an advantage that the gîte d'étape at the Baisse de Camp d'Argent has everything needed for recovery at the end of this long walk. GR52 climbs from 300m in Sospel to 1,900m, before undulating for another 8km towards the Authion. This rounded hill is at the convergence of several ridges, and its proximity to the border has given it strategic importance. This is reflected by a series of ruined hill-top forts and barracks constructed in Napoleonic times. The forts were occupied by invading forces in the 1939-45 war. They were liberated by the First Division of the Free French Army on 11 and 12 April 1945, less than a month before peace was declared in Europe. This liberation was at terrible cost, with 276 Free-French soldiers losing their lives.

A few yards down the road from the hotel a path descends to the right, crosses the zigzagging road twice and then the railway before reaching a road junction and GR52 at [105]. Going north-northwest from there through the southern outskirts of Sospel leads to the river Bévéra. A short distance to the left along the river bank lies a stone bridge with a fortified gateway. The GR crosses the bridge, enters an attractive square in the old town and leaves the square from the left side.

Resting on a massive rusting artillery piece at the Baisse de Linière

After passing signposts [71] and [74] on the road leading northwest out of the old town GR52 becomes a well-made mule track, which makes for easy walking on the first 250m ascent. There is then a short section on a country road to signpost [75], where a path heads northwest, crosses another lane at [76] and then climbs a fine ridge to the Baisse de Linière at 1,342m. At this grassy col a large rusted gun barrel lies in the grass (above) reflecting the extensive defences around the Authion. The path splits at the col with GR52 going to the right along the ridge and then onto its steep western flank. This path crosses the western ridge of the Cime du Ters and then climbs to the summit of the Mangiabo. Next it follows the main crête for a while, before passing to the left of the Cime de la Gonella (below) and reaching the Baisse de la Déa [141], where the path crosses a rough mountain track..

Passing on the west flank of the Cime de la Gonella as the mist rolls in

The main climb of the day is now over and the route continues for a km or so on the east flank of the Pointe de Ventabren (1978m). On reaching the next col the GR crosses the same mountain track encountered earlier and then continues on the gentle western slope of the ridge for another 4 km. At [151] the path joins the track again and the route, for a short time, leaves GR52, continuing to the metaled D68 mountain road at a hairpin bend. The road is followed to the left through a hairpin bend and at the next bend there is a vacherie on the left below the road. Here the route rejoins GR52, following a track that heads northeast just below and parallel to the road. After a while the track becomes a path, which contours the hillside below the road and eventually rejoins the D68 at the Baisse de Camp d'Argent. Then a right turn up the road leads, after 0.14km, to the Gîte d'Étape l'Estive du Mercantour www.estive-mercantour.fr/. This is an excellent lodging house, with a welcoming open fire.

Day 3: Baisse de Camp d'Argent to Ref des Merveilles (2115m)
12.8km, up 1237m, down 850m, high point le Pas du Diable 2432m, 5h00

GR52 heads up the grassy ski run opposite the gîte and soon joins the lane (D68) that leads to a war memorial beside the road at [244]. From there the GR climbs to the crest of the grassy west ridge of the Authion. This crosses over the north summit and continues to [410]. In early summer the slopes on either side of the ridge are covered in flowers including cowslips and orchids. Most poignantly, huge drifts of white pasque flower anemones, provide a reminder of the slaughter of young men that occurred on this hillside at the end of the second world war.

The ridge stretching north from the Authion towards the Cime du Diable

Ahead from [410] lies the ruins of an ancient square fortress. The view north from there looks along a winding ridge (above). This ridge ends at the Cime du Diable with the high point of the day's walk, the Pas du Diable, on its eastern flank. Just before and below this fortress at signpost [410] GR52 continues on a track that descends northwards to the Baisse de St. Véran [409]. When the author passed that way in June 2008 he talked with a shepherd at this baisse, who told him that it had rained almost every day for the previous six weeks. With his dogs the shepherd was enjoying the rare sunshine. It was these weeks of rain that translated into the exceptional snow cover that was encountered later in the day and at high level throughout the Alpes Maritimes during this walk. From the Baisse de St. Véran GR52 continues on the east side of the ridge as a path, climbing sharply to the Col de Raus [406]. There it crosses the ridge and passes onto the steep north-eastern flank of the Cime de Raus. The path then traverses north-eastwards to the Baisse Caveline (2107m). From there it descends some 30m to the floor of the valley and then climbs on its far side to the Pas du Diable, the high point of the day. Compass baring 336° at the pass leads after 0.25km to point [404] between the two small frozen Lacs du Diable (below). There the GR turns to the east and way-marking on large boulders signals the route, first to the north of the Lac de la Muta, then south of the Lac du Trem, finally descending on the south-eastern side of the Lac Fourca to the Refuge des Merveilles www.cafnice.org/site/refuge/merveilles/. This CAF refuge offers dormitory accommodation with multi-berth bunks, good food and cold showers. In June 2008 this was an efficiently managed refuge that was run rather strictly. For example, access to the dormitories and inside toilets was denied before 6 pm.

Looking from the Pas du Diable towards the frozen snow-covered Lacs du Diable

Day 4: Refuge des Merveilles to la Madone de Fenestre (1,903m)
16km, up 1,450m, down 1,678m, high point le Pas de l'Arpette 2,511m, 6h30

The snow conditions made it impracticable in June 2008 to follow GR52 to the Madonne de Fenestre. The steep descent from the Baisse du Basto and the crossing of the equally steep Pas du Mt Colomb would have involved time consuming snow and ice climbing, as well as appropriate equipment. A description of a walk on this magnificent section of GR52 in snow-free conditions in September 2002 is given in Chapter 6. Fortunately, there is an alternative, less steep, but still interesting way south of GR52 to reach the Madonne de Fenestre.

This southern option climbs more or less due west from the refuge to the Pas de l'Arpette. Not surprisingly at 2,511m there was snow in June 2008 on either side of the pass, but this was not steep and posed no technical difficulties.

Traverse of the border alps from the sea

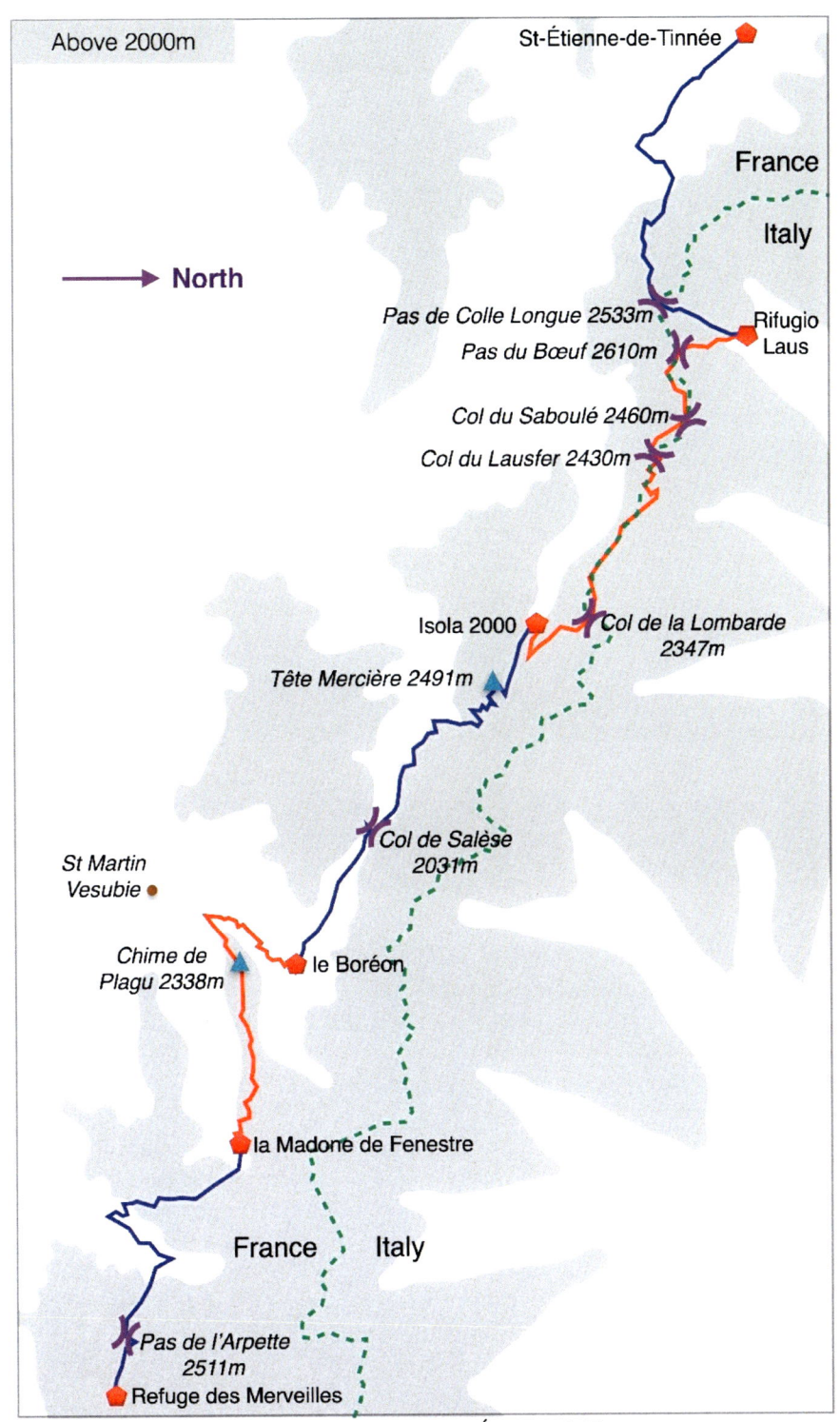

Days 4 to 8 the Refuge de Merveilles to Saint-Étienne-de-Tinée

From the mouth of this upper valley a steep zigzagging path winds down wooded hillside of the Val d'Empuonrame (below) to the D171 road-head at the Pont du Countet. Some 1.5km down the mountain road the Relais des Merveilles (not to be confused with the Refuge des Merveilles the previous night's stopover) provides a pleasant stop for refreshments.

Descent of the Val d'Empuonrame

Further along the road at [275] a steep zigzagging path rises north-westwards up open hillside, gaining some 800m before reaching a ridge northeast of the Baisse de Prals. Here there are fine views of the rock aiguilles that rise to the east of the Madone de Fenestre. To the north, across a valley, lies the hanging valley with its five Lacs de Prals. From the ridge the route heads north-westwards and then just east of north on a path, marked with black dashes on the map. This path leads directly to the lakes, where it threads its way between the two most north-westerly of these before climbing to [366] at the Baisse des Cinq Lacs. It then descends north-north-westwards down the Vallon du Ponset to the chapel and CAF Refuge at la Madone de Fenestre. This large refuge www.cafnice.org/site/refuge/madone/ offers a warm welcome and comfortable bunk accommodation with hot showers. The attractive cluster of buildings, including the refuge, originally housed a monastery, founded in the 12th century by monks of the Benedictine order. It is worth spending a little time visiting the almost cave-like Chapel by the Refuge.

Day 5: la Madone de Fenestre to le Boréon (1,530m)
13.4km, up 1,070m, down 1,474m, high point Cime de Piagu 2,338m, 5hr15

This is a relatively short, but interesting and varied, walk that provides stunning views of the high peaks of the Alps Maritime. The path starts at [356], which is sited southwest of the refuge at the far end of the upper car park. It is the upper of the two paths and zigzags up the steep open hillside to the northwest. After a while the path gradient eases and it starts to traverse for some 3km round the Plage de l'Agnellière, climbing steadily to the Cime du Pisset at 2,233m, the first of the summits to be crossed on the ridge.

The twin peak of the Argentera from the Cime de Piagu

It is another 3 km of easy walking to the high point of the ridge, the Cime de Piagu, with a steep, but short, pull up the last section to the summit. The photo above looks back along the broad ridge towards the frontier peaks with the twin tops of the Argentera, the highest peak in the Alpes Maritime, rising beyond the end of the ridge. From the summit of the Cime de Piagu the path, marked with yellow flashes, descends, at times steeply, on its broad southwest ridge. At [385], which is sited around 550m below the summit and some way after the ridge becomes forested, a right fork traverses back northwards on the Boréon side of the hill. This is also marked with yellow flashes. It is an entertaining route and no gentle walk in the woods, for apart from fallen trees there are significant ascents and descents to avoid rocky outcrops. At [383], a point north of and some 560m below the Cime de Piagu, a left fork heads down through the forest to the road at le Boréon.

Lodging with meals are available at the Gîte d'Étape du Boréon http://giteduboreon.monsite-orange.fr/. This lies a little way up a lane to the right, off the road that leads to the Col Salèse. As the gîte does not open before 16.00 you might want to wait at a pleasant bar/restaurant down the road by the Lac du Boréon.

Day 6: Le Boréon to Isola 2000 (2,050m)
20.2km, up 1,644m, descent 1,112m, high point Tête Mercière 2,491m, 7hr15

This walk briefly rejoins GR52, which passes the gîte and follows the narrow road westwards towards the Col Salèse. At [399], some 1.7km from the gîte the GR descends to the left on a path through the forest to the Boréon Torrent. After crossing this stream by a wooden bridge it continues to the right along the far bank, climbing gently through the woods for some 0.9km. Then the GR crosses the river again by another bridge and reaches the road at a hairpin bend. From there it immediately heads west from the road passing signpost [434] and climbing gently through the woods to the left of the road. Eventually the GR rejoins the road, now surfaced with white gravel, just before the Col Salèse at [135]. It follows the road westwards over the col and then bypasses the next two loops in the road. About half a km from the col at [267] the route takes the right fork away from GR52 onto a track that crosses the valley stream by the Pont d'Ingolf. This pleasant and often grassy track continues, contouring on the north side of the valley at about 2,000m for some 6km through larch forest. At [256] the track starts to ascend in long loops in a generally north-westerly direction, passing some well-preserved military bunkers set into the hillside below the Col de Mercière. It is worth making a detour here, climbing westward across the alp to the high point on the ridge, the Tête Mercière (2491m). The view from there to the east looks towards the border hills (below) while northwards lies Isola 2000 and beyond the frontier ridge.

The summit of the Tête Mercière with the frontier ridge behind

Until 1945 the high valley holding Isola 2000 was an Italian, royal hunting ground. This was ceded to the French at the end of hostilities. It was then a summer pasture until the ski station was built through the entrepreneurial initiative of a British army officer, Peter Boumphrey. The resort was opened in 1971. Isola 2000 lies 1,120m above and 15km from the small ancient village of Isola, on the north bank of the River Tinée.

After descending east to the Col Mercière [95] the route heads down into Isola 2000, passing a small reservoir before reaching the high-rise holiday apartment blocks of the resort. In June Isola 2000 is between seasons and more or less closed. None of the hotels are available and there is no gîte d'ètape. A solution is to rent a studio for the night. A local estate agent at the Agence de Colombe www.decolombe.com/ will organise this. Generally a simple restaurant is open in the evening to serve maintenance workers in the resort.

Day 7: Isola 2000 to Rifugio del Laus (1,913m)
20.8km, ascent 1,884m, descent 1,900 m, high point Tete Rougnous 2,694m, 8h30

This is one of the best walks between Menton and Briançon once the Col de la Lombarde has been reached. The route from there follows the Italian/French border ridge in a generally westerly direction, crossing some magnificent, but challenging terrain.

It seems logical to follow the footpath to the east of the road that leads to the Col de la Lombarde. On the other hand, excoriations made by ski resort machines and lack of use make route finding along this off-road route difficult. Consequently there is a good case for walking up the road to the Col de la Lombarde to get straight to the delights that follow.

The Lac di Colle di Santa Anna

At the col the route passes into Italy and unfortunately is no longer marked on the latest IGN 1:25k map (October 2017). Older versions show the path on adjacent Italian territory. From the road at the col a track heads up left from the road towards the border ridge, traversing across the base of the northern flank of the Tête de l'Adrech d'en Barris. At this stage the ridge is broad and grassy and is easy walking. Little plaques are set in the ground to mark the French frontier with Italy. After 2.5km Monte Viso comes into view lying some 50km further north at the edge of the Queyras Alps. At 3,841m this peak stands well above all its neighbours.

After this viewpoint the path descends on the Italian side of the border between rocks, losing some 250m before reaching the Lac di Colle di Santa Anna (photo previous page). At the far side of this pretty tarn a twisting track paved with stone climbs back up to the border ridge at the Pas Sainte Anne. Through the pass there is a fine view south-westwards to the cone of Mont Mounier, a prominent peak of the Alpes d'Haut Provence. The path through the col leads down to Isola, but our route follows a track that winds round the head-wall of a north-facing Italian cirque to the Col de Lausfer.

Kicking steps across the north-facing Italian cirque on the way to the Col de Lausfer.

Halfway between the cols there is a prominent rocky spur that divides this cirque. In June 2008 most of both sections of the cirque were covered by steep snow (above), which obliterated the track. Fortunately the run-out from these snow-covered slopes was generally gentle, making the long traverse kicking steps relatively safe, but the author was still glad to have his ice axe.

From the Col du Lausfer [65] the path descends on the French side of the border to [65a]. There the path to the right climbs above the three little Lacs Lausfer Inferieurs over a low col to the larger Lac Lausfer Superieur. After passing this lake on its south-western side the path climbs gently to the Col de Saboulé at the frontier ridge [64]. Then the path again crosses into Italy, heads northwest past some ruined fortifications before crossing back over the border.

156

Now the route traverses westwards under the south face of the Roche du Saboulé. There is no semblance of a path, although some cairns mark a way up open mountainside to the ridge that links the Cime de Prals with the 2,685m point on the border ridge. From there an airy, but delightful, rocky ridge leads to the high point of the day, the Tete Rougnous (below).

Looking back along the border ridge from the summit of the Tete Rougnous (2,694m)

From this summit the ridge descends west-northwest to point 2,610m, from where there is no way forward, for the international border plunges precipitously to La Col de la Guercha. The solution is still tricky and involves descending right into Italy to a visible stony path that leads westwards up to the Pas du Bœuf (Passo del Bue). This is a breach 0.1km along a sharp rocky ridge that runs north from the frontier. It is NOT on the frontier ridge as implied on the recently-modified IGN 1.25k map (current October 2017 on the geoportail website). The descent from this pass is seriously exposed and should only be tackled in good conditions by experienced walkers with a good head for heights. The way down follows a series of narrow and exposed ledges (photo page 142). These lead to a zigzagging "path" on steep, slippery scree of fragmented slate that eventually comes to safer ground in the Vallone della Guercia. An alternative to this delicate section heads east from the approach to the Pas du Boeuf on a path that winds round to the north into the Vallone della Sauma and then leads to the road to St Bernolfo, 280m below the Rifugio del Laus. This alternative would add about an hour and a half to an already-long day.

From the Valone della Guercha it is a relatively straightforward walk to the Lago San Bernolfo, although this can be complicated by snow cover on the final descent to the lake. The ochre-painted Rifugio del Laus www.rifugiolaus.it lies just over the col on the west side of this lake. Normally the rifugio only opens on Saturdays and Sundays outside July and August unless a prior booking is made.

Day 8: Rifugio del Laus to St-Étienne-de-Tinée (1,145m)
17km, up 776m, down 1,637m, high point the Pas de Colle Longue 2,533m, 5h00

This walk starts on a well-made stony track heading west-south-westwards up the Vallone di Collalunga. In June 2008 at higher levels the track was covered with snow, which continued up to the border. Just after the frontier there is a hollow with two small lakes to the right (below), which are passed before reaching the high point of the day, the Pas de Colle Longue [59a].

Les Lacs de Colle Longue beneath the Roca di San Bernolfo

The southern, French side, of the border was largely snow-free, with rusting barbed wire scattered on the surrounding grass, presumably a remnant of border defences of the 1939-1945 war. Gradually the path moves onto a steep south-facing incline and slowly descends south-westwards until it reaches a gently sloping meadow at point 2,403m. From there the path heads west for 1.5km before turning sharply east-northeast as it crosses a ridge and winds round the back of a pretty hanging valley, with a small lake at its base. The path then zigzags down steep floral meadows, eventually reaching a lane (D62) that descends to the main D2205 road up the Tinée Valley. On the far side of this road there is a walking/cycle track which is followed into St Étienne. After the Tinée road bridge the cycle track leaves the main road and runs along a lane to the right through fields between the main road and the river. Half way to St Étienne this lane is joined by GR5. The Gîte d'Étape le Corborant www.gite-tinee-mercantour.com/ is on the GR5 at the entrance to St Étienne de Tinée. Both St Étienne, with its old buildings and narrow streets, as well as its gîte d'étape, are worth a visit.

Traverse of the border alps from the sea

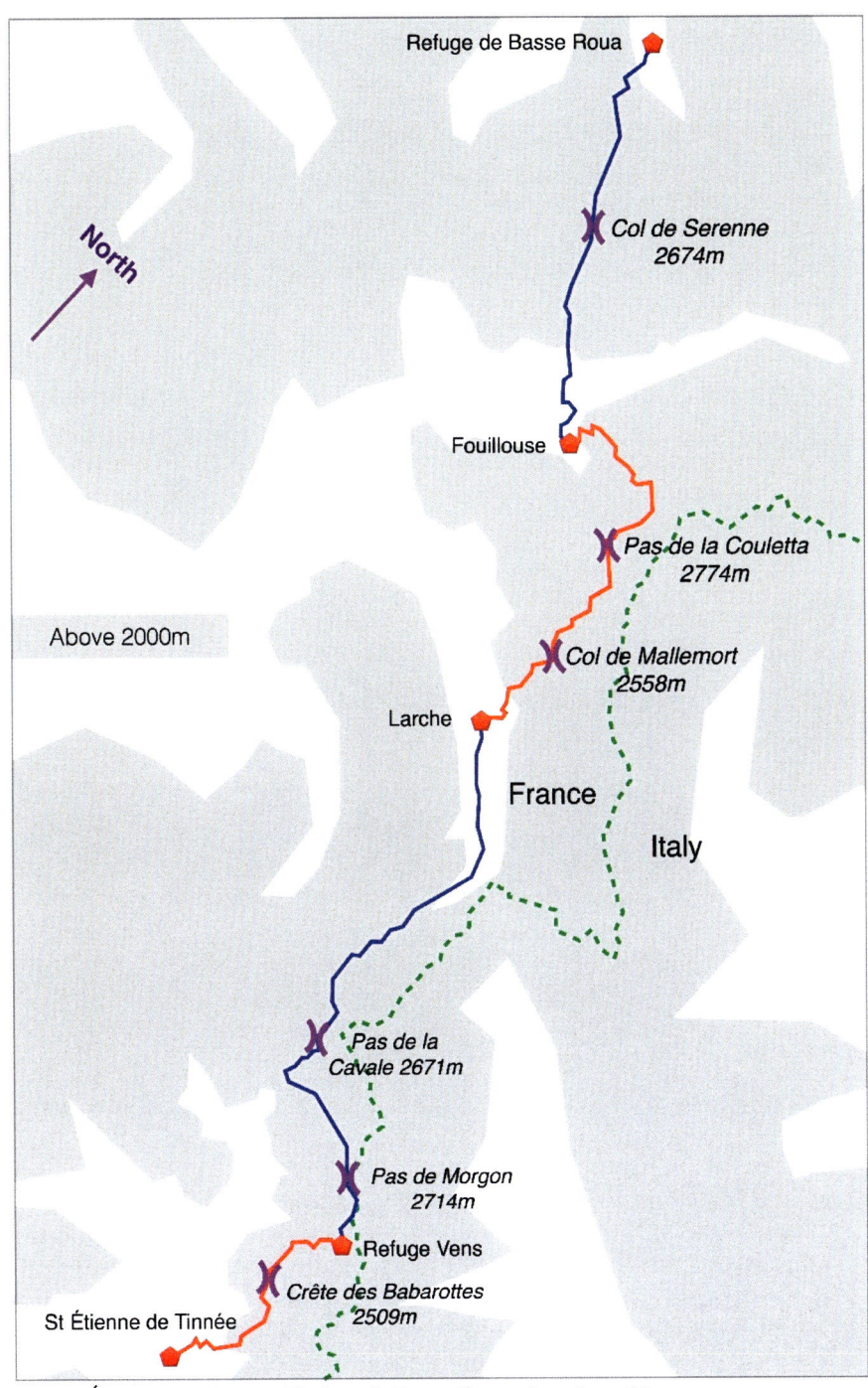

Saint-Étienne-de-Tinée to Refuge de Basse Roua days 9 to 12

Day 9: St-Étienne-de-Tinée to the Refuge de Vens (2,380m)
10.8km, up 1,814m, down 607m, high point Crête des Babarottes 2,509m, 5h30

Although this day's walk is relatively short it involves a steep, long ascent from the Tinée valley to the Chemin de l'Énergie. The chemin is a track that runs horizontally along the northern wall of the Tinée valley at about 2,300m. It was built for an ambitious hydroelectric project in the first decade of the 20th century, but the project was halted by the First World War and never finished. The beauty of the lakes on the approach to the Refuge de Vens and the hills that surround the refuge make this a walk to savour rather than rush.

St-Étienne-de-Tinée from the steep path to the Chemin de l'Énergie

Leaving GR5 in the old town the route goes through the narrow streets to the bridge at the northeast corner of St-Étienne. On the far side of the bridge a left turn up the road leads, after a few metres, to signpost [108]. There a path to the right is followed that zigzags steeply up to the north gaining 600m altitude before crossing a path at [109]. The photo above looks back to St Étienne from this path, which continues to zigzag upwards after [109] until it reaches the Chemin de l'Énergie and the Mercantour Park border at signpost [112]. The chemin provides a fast route along the north side of the Tinée valley, but in early summer steep snow-filled gullies, with outruns that become very steep, may provide objective danger (below). An ice axe and instep crampons may assist in crossing these obstacles with reasonable confidence. Finally the chemin peters out in a boulder field. Here at [113] a path going just west of north crosses the boulders and climbs to the Crête des Babarottes.

A steep snow gully on the Chemin de l'Énergie; no place for a slip

Once over the ridge the path descends to the Lac des Babarottes and passes on its left shore before descending to the lowest of les Lacs de Vens. After passing between this lake and the next, the path crosses the outflow from the latter by a wooden bridge. A profusion of brilliant sky-blue trumpet gentians cover the alp on the far side of the bridge in late June. The path next passes to the northwest of three more lakes and then climbs a granite headland that separates the highest and largest of the lakes from its neighbours.

The Refuge de Vens lies at the head of the top lake on a rocky outcrop between two waterfalls. This is another refuge run by the Nice branch of the CAF www.cafnice.org/site/refuge/vens/. As with most CAF refuges a booking can be made and the deposit paid on line. The wonderful location of the hut gives it majestic views from the terrace.

Day 10: Refuge de Vens to Larche (1,666m)
22.6km, up 1,175m, down 1,849m, high point Pas de Morgon 2,714m, 7h30

A substantial portion of this walk crosses unmarked trackless ground. Navigation skills are required, but the ground covered is not technically difficult, with the exception of a short section of steep snow encountered in early summer on the final approach to the Pas de Morgan (below).

From the refuge the path that heads north-northwest in long zigzags is followed to the Collet de Tortisse [35a]. Southwest along the ridge from this col are bizarrely shaped rock outcrops – the Aiguilles de Tortisse. The route heads in the opposite direction to the Col de Fer and the Italian border. At the col there is a fine view into Italy with the unmistakable split cone of Monte Viso visible in the background.

The snow wall defending the final approach to the Pas de Morgan

At the Col de Fer the route leaves marked paths and heads north and then north-west up the frontier ridge to the Pas de Morgan. At first this is along an interesting and varied crest. Despite considerable snow the ridge presented no difficulties in late June apart from a short climb up steep snow on the final approach to the pass (above). The route onwards is truly trackless. The goal is the Pas de la Cavale (2671m). If the weather is clear this can be pinpointed at baring 305° on the far side of the valley above the place where grass continues almost two thirds of the way up the steep scree slope below the pass.

Despite the lack of a recognised path the way onwards from the Pas de Morgon to GR5 at the base of the Pas de la Cavale is straightforward. It more or less follows the left-hand of two ski-touring routes from the Pas de Morgon that are marked on the IGN map. Start this section of the walk on compass baring 306º, which leads after 0.6km to some small lakes. Pass to the right of these and then on baring 285 º continue to the left side of a stream. This leads across increasingly grassy slopes, gradually winding round to the west. In places the slope is steep, but not difficult if the line of least resistance is selected. After crossing the main valley stream the aim is to reach [37] and GR5. The GR is clearly way-marked with red and white flashes. If one comes to the path that runs north-westwards from [37] to the Col de Pouriac the lack of such way-marks will indicate that it is necessary to head down the path to reach GR5.

More snow fields on the way forward from the Pas de la Cavale

The way northwards from [37] on GR5 zigzags up grassy alp passing above and to the left of the small Lacs d'Agnel. Higher up the grassy buttress peters out and the way ahead crosses steep scree. This leads to a fractured rock wall that looks challenging. Somehow a way opens up so the final ascent to the Pas de Cavale is spectacular, but not difficult, despite the magenta dots on the map.

From the Pas de la Cavale there is a long descent of the Vallon du Lauzanier. At first this may involve crossing large, but not threatening snow slopes (above) on the way to the upper lake, the Lac de Derrière la Croix. Ahead in the distance lie the Chambeyron hills, where the walk continues on day 11.

Further down, below the first two lakes green alp surrounds the Lac du Lauzanier (below). After this lake the path descends to a less scenic lower valley, known as Val Fourane. In the flat bottom of this valley the path becomes a track, which some 2.5km further on passes into a car park.

GR5 exits to the left from the car park on a lane that gradually winds round to the northwest following the left flank of the valley of the Ubayette for 3.5km. The road and GR5 then cross the River Ubayette and join the main road from the Col de Larch and Italy. The small village of Larche lies one km down this road. Excellent accommodation and food are available at the Gîte d'Étape Grand Traversée des Alps www.gite-etape-larche.com/. This is on the left at the entrance to the village. The wall of the gîte facing the road and the side walls are metal clad and painted grey. By contrast the southern side, facing the river, has a pleasant wooden facade fronted by a lawn with tables.

The verdant surrounds of the Lac du Lauzanier

Day 11: Larche to Fouillouse (1,872m)
18.4km, up 1,639m, down 1,444m, high point Pas de la Couletta 2,774m, 7h15

The route from Larch starts on the GR5, zigzagging up the open alp north of the village and gaining almost 1,000m before reaching the Col de Mallemort at 2,558m. Just over this col the path passes to the right of les Baraquements de Viraysse. These ruined barracks date from 1882 and lie at the south end of a fine high valley, which is surrounded by a series of rocky pointed peaks. On the far side of the ruins GR5 gradually descends north-north-westwards. Then from a right fork it heads north-north-eastwards, crosses a stream and from there climbs northwards to the Col du Vallonet. Here GR5 takes the line of least resistance to the left, but our route follows a path to the right that heads past the north side of the Lac du Vallonnet Superieur. From there the path winds counter clockwise round a knoll, the Tête de Plate Lombarde. At the north-eastern end of this knoll, a left fork heads north-westwards for a further 1.4 km. Then, a right turn climbs just east of north up beautiful alp to the highest point on the walk from Menton to Briançon, the Pas de la Couletta (below). The rock tower of the Brec de Chambeyron dominates the eastern flank of the pass, while the elegant Aiguille de Chambeyron, the highest peak in these hills, rises on the other side of the high valley ahead. Just after the pass a left fork descends steeply on a slate scree path, past the east side of the milky green Lac Premier to the Refuge de Chambeyron. The path onwards then traverses under the Bec Roux descending westwards to Fouillouse.

The approach to the Pas de la Couletta with the Brec de Chambeyron in the background

In this pretty village, with shingle-roofed houses, the Gîte les Granges www.gitelesgranges.com/en/ is located on the right at the lower end of the sloping cobbled street. This popular gîte was full when the author visited it despite it being a Monday in June. It is wise to book.

Day 12: Fouillouse to Refuge de Basse Rua (1,760m)
15.8km, up 1,342m, down 1,454m, high point the Col de Serenne 2,674m, 6h15

The way on from Fouillouse starts on the GR5, heading right from the road at the bottom of the village. The path traverses for a while before climbing round the lip of a cirque. It then enters woods and descends to the road that links

Fouillouse with the Ubaye valley. This road leads down to the spectacular Pont du Châtelet, which spans the high vertical rock walls of the gorge of the River Ubaye.

Some 0.2km beyond the bridge the road joins the D25. A little under half a km to the right, the road crosses a bridge over the torrent that flows from the Vallon du Châtelet. Just after this bridge the route leaves GR5 and follows a path that leaves to the left, passing an old lime kiln and climbing steeply to the right of the torrent. Beyond a shack built against a boulder, marked on the map as the Cabane Sous le Rocher, the valley opens up into grassy meadow and is now termed the Vallon de Serenne. Here the path, way-marked with orange flashes, continues up the right side of the valley stream to the Col de Serenne.

The snow-capped peaks of the Écrins come into view from the Col de Serenne

From the col the path gently descends the wide and grassy Vallon Laugier, the snow-capped eastern peaks of the Écrins forming the background (above). After passing to the left of a bergerie the path crosses the stream and continues to the end of the hanging Laugier valley. There is then a steep descent of the headwall through woods to the floor of the main Escreins Valley. The path then runs over the dry stone bed to the left of the river. On reaching a track this is followed across a bridge over the river to the Refuge de Basse Rua www.refuge-basserua.fr/. This excellent modern refuge, run by Eric Disdier, is delightfully situated. It offers everything the walker could want.

Day 13: Refuge de Basse Rua to Ceillac (1,636m)
15.8km, up 1,778m, down 1,890m, high point the Pic d'Escreins 2,734m, 7h00

This challenging, but delightful walk crosses the jagged peaks that separate the Escreins and Ceillac valleys. The route is on what used to be called GR58, but

Traverse of the border alps from the sea

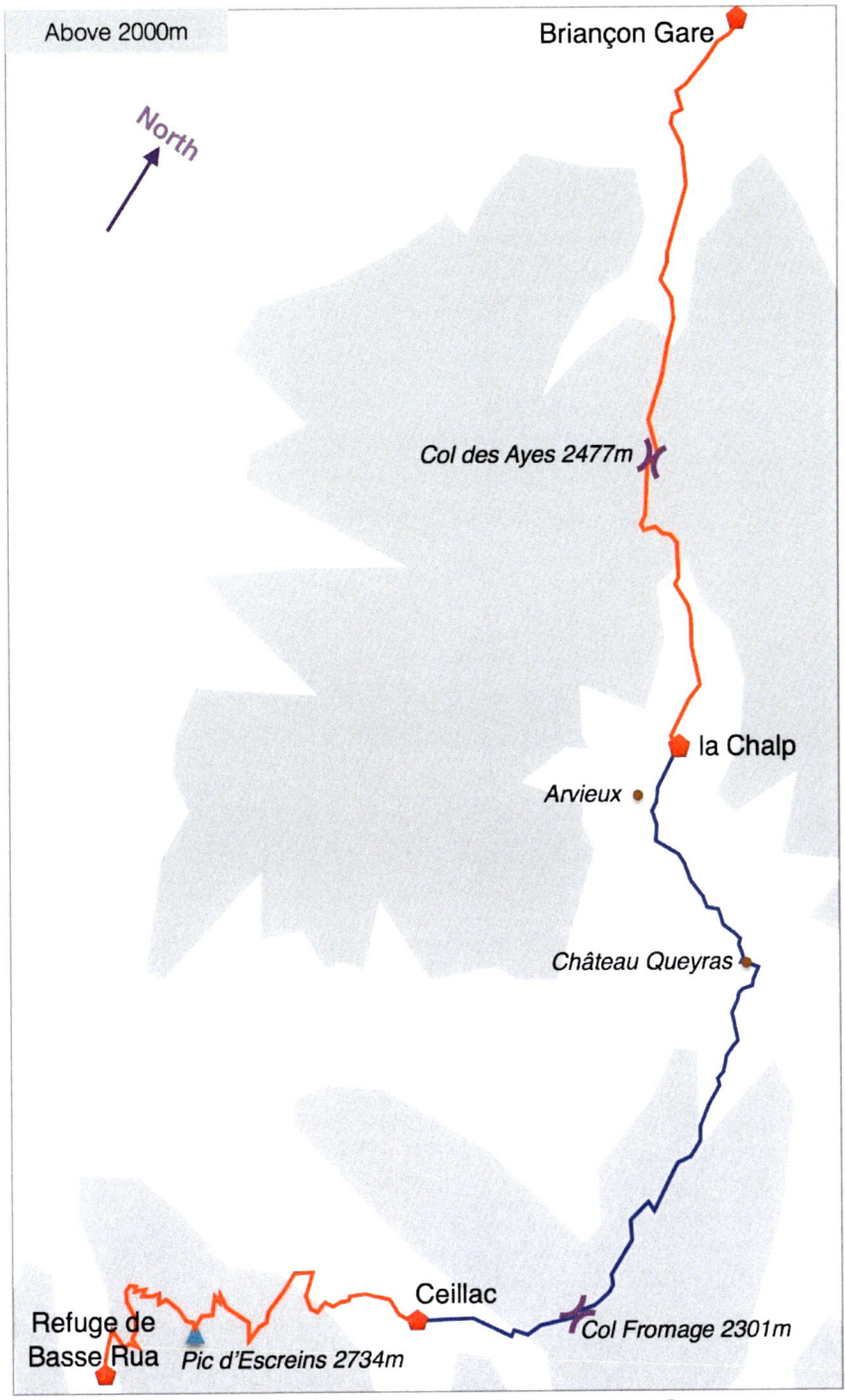

Menton to Briançon the last 3 days Refuge de Basse Rua to Briançon Gare

Mountains of the Provençal Rim

now forms one third of a three-day circuit, the GR de Pays: du Tour de la Font Sancte. A second day of this delectable circuit is described in day 11 of Chapter 2 in this book. The section from the Refuge de Basse Rua to Ceillac, described here, provides an interesting and airy route up the cliffs to the north of the refuge. There are some metal steps and fixed ropes to protect in tricky places. On reaching the top of the cliff there is a long traverse to the west, to a point where a broad path climbs in long zigzags to a col just below and to the north of the summit of the Pic d'Escreins. It is worth making a short detour to this summit, which is a magnificent view point (below).

Les Pics de la Font Sancte from the Pic d'Escreins

After returning to the col the GR descends eastwards into a large stony bowl. From the base of this hollow the path turns north and climbs onto the Crête d'Andreveysson. This ridge is grassy at the start, but then becomes an airy white grit buttress. The GR leads down the buttress to a point where a steep gully provides a safe means to descend the cliffs to the right of the crête and reach the Vallon des Pelouses. This vallon is indeed covered with lush green grass in early summer and the route across the valley is marked by short wooden posts with red and white bands on the top. These lead past the south side of the Bergerie Andrevez and into a horizontal grassy lateral-valley, where there is a way-mark on some slabs to the left of the path. From the exit of the valley the GR climbs up to the right gaining some 120m before contouring on the steep wall of the Créte de la Mourière. It is important not to be seduced by a well-trodden path that descends from the end of the lateral valley and then traverses right before petering out in a steep trackless cwm with scrub-covered walls. At the north end of the crête de la Mourière there is a Belvedere where Ceillac comes into view 600m below. The remainder of the walk descends on a good stony path, still way-marked with red and white flashes, to this large village. At the southern edge of old Ceillac lies the Gîte d'Étape Les Baladins www.baladins.queyras.com. It is yet another excellent lodging house. Spend some time exploring the village with its interesting ancient wooden houses.

Château Queyras seen from GR5 on the approach from the south

Day 14: Ceillac to La Chalp d'Arvieux (1,678m)
20.1km, up 1,589m, down 1,622m, high point the Col Fromage 2,301m, 7h30

The route on the last two days before Briançon faithfully follows GR5 and is predictably relatively easy going, but of continued interest. This leaves Ceillac on a lane heading northeast and soon follows a path diagonally up the hillside to the left. After passing the Chapel Ste. Barbe there is a division of paths and GR5 continues north-eastwards, climbing on a well-graded and partially-shaded path to the Col Fromage. At the col the path heads northwards contouring below the Crête de la Selle and then through the edge of forestry. Some 2.5km from the col the path crosses a broad ridge and then descends in zigzags into a valley labelled the Pré Faure on the map. The GR flashes assist route finding down this valley, for cattle have created additional tracks that would otherwise make it difficult to identify the correct way. Eventually the Château Queyras comes into view (above). This is an impressive fortification sited on top of a rocky outcrop that rises on the north side of the River Guil.

GR5 crosses the river on a road bridge and then climbs up through the village to the main road, which is followed westwards. After passing the château and continuing on the road through one loop the GR heads north from the road climbing steeply in zigzags through pine woods. Eventually it reaches the south end of the Lac de Roue, a good place on a hot day for a rest in the shade of surrounding trees. From the lake the route descends to les Maisons through exquisite fields, filled in early summer with wild flowers. After skirting to the east side of this hamlet the GR traverses northwards through woods above the village of Arvieux and on to la Chalp and the Gîte d'Étape/Chambre d'Hôte le Chalet Viso www.chaletviso.com. This spacious gîte is an excellent stopover.

The flower-filled meadows on the descent to the Chalets des Ayes

Day 15: La Chalp d'Arvieux to Briançon Gare(1,203m)
19.1km, up 978m, down 1,440m, high point the Col des Ayes 2,477m, 6h15

The start of the last day's the walk to Briançon follows the road from la Chalp towards the Col d'Izoard. After a few minutes and just before the village of Brunissard, a lane to the left leads north-westwards for 3 km to a car park. From there GR5 continues on a track that goes through 3 bends before reaching a large flat grassy area – la Pré Premier. This is surrounded by hills and has a lake at its far end. Here GR5 continues up a track that climbs from the right side of the meadow. After the track rounds the southwest ridge of a hill it flattens off in alpine meadows. Now a signpost indicates GR5 leading to the right up grassy slopes to the Col des Ayes, the last high pass before Briançon.

The descent through beautiful floral meadows (above) passes the two Chalets de Vers le Col on the way to the Chalets des Ayes. The lane running through this village continues along the base of the valley, splitting about a km after the last house. Here the route follows the higher left fork on a track that traverses through forest still towards the north-northwest. Where the track winds round to the west GR5 descends northwards on a path to a lane that zigzags down to Sachas.

From this village GR5 makes a somewhat artificial detour to the east and back. It is probably better to walk the 2km to Briançon railway station on the road. There are several reasonably-priced hotels near the station. If you are staying the night and are not too exhausted walk the 1.5km up to the old fortified town. It is well worth a visit.

Return from Briançon

From Briançon trains run via Gap to Marseille, Aix-en-Provence, Lyon and Grenoble. There is also a bus service to Grenoble and Lyon airport.

Crossing the outflow from les Lacs de Vans Day 9

An inquisitive marmot in the Mercantour National Park

8 CHAPTER
HIGH PASSES OF THE SOUTHERN ÉCRINS
Two circular walks from les Borels totaling 116.9km with 8,591m ascent

To the south of the glaciated peaks of the Écrins and northwest of the River Durance lie a series of remote passes over ridges that separate the valleys of the Southern Écrins. This excellent 7 day walk, was completed in September 2016. It comprises two circuits from les Borels, a small village in the Champoléon, the geographically-large commune in the drainage area of the river Drac Blanc.

The first day joins GR50, climbing southwards up the steep western flank of the valley of the Drac Blanc to an airy path above the Aiguilles du Pertuis. The GR then descends to the hamlet of les Richards, which is perched on a spur high above and to the west of the confluence of the Drac Blanc with the Drac Noir. Next the path turns to the west and traverses on the northern flank of the Drac valley to the village of les Marrons. The following day the route heads north, climbing steadily to the Col de Clémens, set in the south ridge of the Vieux Chaillol. There is then a long descent of the remote, steep-sided Tourrond Valley that returns to les Borels.

The five day circuit starts climbing steadily along the southern flank of the Drac valley to le Couchon, a pass set in the west ridge of the Petit Autane. On the far side the path descends to the Rouanne Torrent and follows this to the village of Ancelle. Next the route climbs eastwards to the Col de la Pourrachière and then scales the conical summit of the Piolit. From this peak there are uninterrupted views across the Lac Serre Ponçon to the Alpes d'Haute Provence. After descending the east ridge of the Piolit the route traverses northwards beneath the Pointe de Fleurendon, before climbing to the Col de la Coupa and then descending eastwards to the hamlet of les Gourniers. The following day the walk heads up the gorge-like Chargès valley to the Col de la Règue. At 2,701m, this is the highest point of the whole walk. There is then a descent to an isolated mountain gîte, les Charançons, which lies in forest at the base of a remote steep-walled valley. The penultimate day's route climbs a magnificent, south-facing hillside to another lonely high pass, the Col des Tourettes. From there the route descends through a series of hanging valleys to the delightful ancient village of Prapic, which lies above the road-head at the end of the Drac Noir valley. Finally the return to les Borels walks through forest and beautiful floral alp high on the south side of the valley of the Drac Noir. Eventually the route meets GR50, which leads down to and across the river on the way back to les Borels.

Sunrise on the hills north of les Borels

Details of the Southern Écrins walk

Day 1: les Borels (1,273m) to les Marrons (1,427m)
15.0km, up 1,305m, down 1,152m, high point above Aiguilles du Pertuis 1,869m, 5h49

Day 2: les Marrons to les Borels (1,273m)
16.3km, up 1,308m, down 1,467m, high point Col de Clémens 2,487m, 6h15

Day 3: les Borels to Ancelle (1,345m)
21.9km, up 1,268m, down 1,200m, high point le Cuchon 2,002, 7h09

Day 4: Ancelle to Gîte des Tris Cols les Gourniers (1,477m)
16.1km, up 1,350m, down 1,200m, high point the Col de la Coupa 2,323m, 6h05
including the ascent of le Piolit
22.7km, up 1,870m, down 1,720m, high point le Piolit 2,484m, 8h36

Day 5: les Gourniers to Gîte d'Étape les Charançons (1,575m)
15.0km, up 1,448m, down 1,339m, high point Col de la Règue 2,706m, 6h08

Day 6: les Charançons to Prapic (1,562m)
14.8km, up 1,188m, down 1,218m, high point Col des Tourettes 2,582m, 5h37

Day 7: Prapic to les Borels (1,273m)
17.8km, up 724m, down 972m, high point at Girardet 1,650m, 5hr

Total distance 116.9km, total ascent 8,591m, daily average 16.7km, 1,227m ascent

Looking northwestwards towards the distant Vieux Chiallol during the descent on Day 6

Mountains of the Provençal Rim

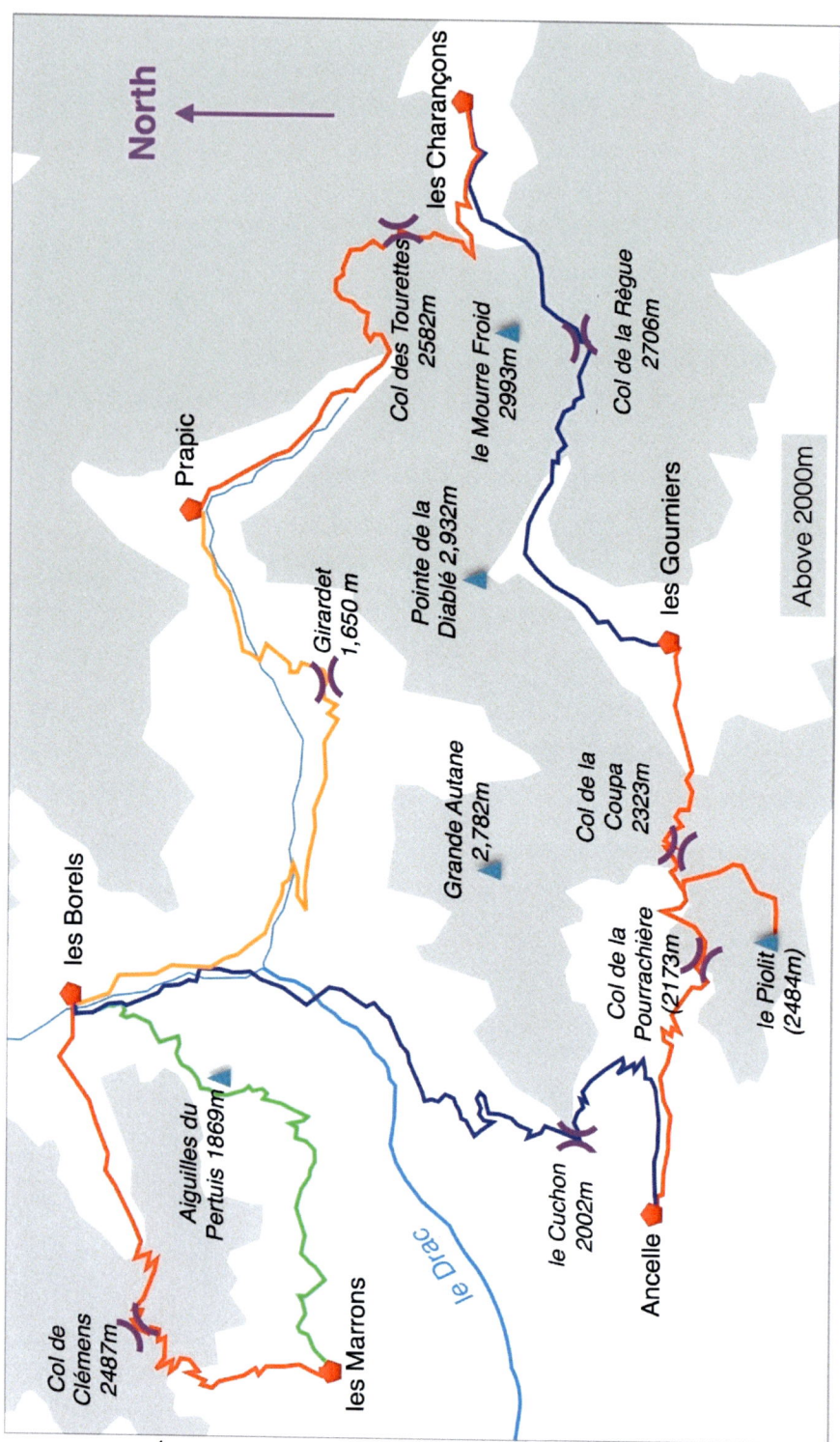

The Southern Écrins Circuits

Journey to les Borels (1,273m)

All of the other walks described in this book use public transport to reach the start. Exceptionally, for walkers coming from the UK, it is more practical to pick up a hire car at Lyon Airport for the 2 hour 45 minute drive via Grenoble and Corps to les Borels. Alternatively, the nearest main line rail station is Gap, from where infrequent busses run the 17km to Ancelle, the stopover on the third night. The Auberge des Écrins www.aubergedesecrins.com, is in the small village of les Borels on the east bank of the River Drac Blanc. The auberge has large family rooms as well as singles and doubles. The meals provided in the half board rate were excellent. There is a spacious carpark at the edge of the village by the Drac Blanc, where a car can be left for several days at no charge.

An airy section of GR50 on the steep western flank of the Drac Blanc

Day 1: les Borels to les Marrons (1,427m)

15.0km, up 1,305m, down 1,152m, high point Aiguilles du Pertuis 1,869m, 5h49

This beautiful and varied walk passes through the mixed woodland on the steep western escarpment of the Drac Blanc. It follows GR50 and in places becomes quite exciting (above). Near the high point of the day, the GR delicately crosses above the Aiguilles du Pertuis, on hillside that is too steep to carry forest. The river at this point tumbles some 2100ft below in the valley floor. GR 50, which is encountered a number of times during this seven-day tour, is a 379km long

Grande Randonnée that encircles the Écrins, generally remaining at between 1,000m and 2,000m above sea level.

The way down to les Richards on GR50

The walk starts on a footpath, labelled on the map as the Tour de Vieux Chaillol. This runs past the west side of the bridge over the Drac Blanc, which lies beyond the entrance to the village. Some 0.8km southwards a right fork starts the climb up the valley escarpment. After a series of zigzags the path straightens out for a while before joining GR50, which comes up from the left. The combined path climbs in a further series of short zigzags, traverses for 0.7km and then goes through a third series of zigzags that lead to the delicate traverse above the Aiguilles du Pertuis. After descending to more level ground the path passes a wooden water trough and then starts to descend southwards. The route now briefly joins a track, but soon leaves for a path to the right. On reaching forest GR50 starts a steep descent in zigzags to a lane that leads through meadows to the hamlet of les Richards (above). This village stands proud on a promontory projecting from the escarpment, with the floor of the broad Champsaur Valley and the river Drac some 1,300ft below. At the end of the village the GR, as a path, circles clockwise through steep pasture round the end of the promontory, before entering sparse forest and winding down to a track. This loops round a cirque and on the far side the GR follows a path to the left that zigzags down through forest above the village of les Bonnets. As the route approaches its low point (1,366m) the path passes through a couple of alarmingly steep granite boulder fields (below), where it would be unfortunate if the hard rock medicine balls started to move.

One of the steep granite boulder fields above les Bonnets

The path then climbs steadily west-northwest to 1,445m. Since 2015 GR50 has been diverted at this point from the path still shown on the 2017 IGN map, because of rock falls. It now heads west on a lower path to the buildings at les Roranches. It then continues west on a track, passing a small church before descending to a stream. Now the track heads southwest and soon a broad grassy path leaves to the right that climbs to rejoin GR50 at 1,603m. The way to les Marrons, on the other hand, continues on an undulating course to the southwest, passing to the north of le Vernet. On coming to a T junction with another path a right turn heads north-northwest and after crossing a stream continues to the west, climbing to join a track on a ridge at 1,573m. This track is followed to the left for 0.1km before turning downhill to the right on a grassy path that continues down to a road just above the village of les Marrons. The Gîte le Chamois lies on the right a short distance down the lane http://www.gite-05-chamois.fr. You will be given a warm welcome at this excellent gîte, set in a pleasant garden. It has comfortable bunks, hot showers and an inside toilet. The four-course evening meal provided by Brigitte is abundant and tasty. This gîte is exceptional value.

Mountains of the Provençal Rim

Day 2: les Marrons to les Borels (1,273m)
16.3km, up 1,308m, down 1,467m, high point Col de Clémens 2,487m, 6h15

This is a great walk over the Col de Clémens back to the Champoléon. The col is set in the southern ridge of the Vieux Chaillol and lies just below and to the right of the left-hand peak in the photograph below.

Looking up towards the Col de Clémens in southern ridge of the Vieux Chaillol

The start returns up the lane leading to the northeast and, after the last house, takes a delightful track that heads north-westwards past the end of a barn and then winds round to the north following a row of trees between two fields. There are fine views from here of the Campsaur and the limestone peaks of the Dévoluy to the west. The path continues to climb gently on the west side of a ridge, with dense coppiced beech woods to the right and open ground to the left. Eventually the path doubles back to the right passing across a rocky gully and climbing to rejoin GR50. The route then traverses left on the GR through trees and at the edge of the wood leaves the GR for a path that climbs gradually in long zigzags north-eastwards through forest. After coming out onto open ground the path continues to climb in zigzags and although the hillside becomes steep the path itself is well graded and maintains a gentle incline. A right fork at the next junction climbs through one more zigzag to another path junction, where a further right turn leads onto the path that climbs to the Col de Clémens (below).

The view northeastwards from the Col de Clémens

Initially, the descent from the col down to the delectable Tourond valley is relatively gentle and after a few zigzags the path makes a long traverse to the southwest. It then turns to the north and zigzags down steep grass above the precipitous cliffs of the Côtes de la Venasque. The path next ingeniously makes its way down these cliffs and in good conditions is quite safe. At the base of the cliffs the path continues to descend, zigzagging through alpine meadow before descending on the damp, wooded and steep southern side of the gorge below the Cascade de la Pisse. The path reaches the south bank of the river, where the Refuge du Tourond lies a short way up the opposite side of the valley. The route continues to the right of the stream following an uncertain track. In places this has been washed away by flash-flooding of side gullies. There is some undulation of the track as it makes its long descent on the wooded south wall of the valley. Where the track starts to curve round to the right and descend steeply there is a notice advising walkers to take a steep narrow zigzagging path to the right that bypasses sections of track that have fallen, or are threatening to fall, into the valley. Eventually, after returning to the track, this swings round to the north for a while before heading east across open ground and passing a picnic area. The track then reaches the bridge over the Drac Blanc, which is crossed to reenter les Borels.

Day 3: les Borels to Ancelle (1,345m)
21.4km, up 1,246m, down 1,179m, high point le Cuchon 2,002m, 6h55

As on the first morning, the route crosses the bridge outside the village and follows the west bank of the river downstream. Instead of following the Tour de Vieux Chaillol up the escarpment this walk continues a short distance above the river for 2.7km until it joins a lane that leads to a lower bridge across the Drac Blanc. On the far side of the river the route heads down the valley on the D499a and then the D944 for a total of 2.3km. Then it turns to the left across the bridge signed to les Ricous. At the start of this village a right turn, southwards, is taken down a lane. After crossing an irrigation canal, a stony track is followed to the left that climbs gently south-westwards through woods.

Across the Champsaur valley towards Caillol and the Eastern Dévoluy

This soon becomes a delightful broad path through beech woods with leaf litter underfoot. The path climbs steadily, in places winding between rocks. Eventually, just before reaching a clearing, the route follows a twisting path to the left through a narrow gate, climbing steeply south-south-eastwards, in the edge of the wood and winding between boulders. Shortly after passing through a second narrow gate the path reaches a broad well-made forest track, which is followed west-south-westwards. At a number of forks, the higher left way is taken. Eventually after the track goes through a hairpin bend and winds round to the east the route turns right at the next fork, onto a track that climbs south-westwards to a belvedere at 1,756m. There are fine views from there across the Champsaur to the hills walked during the previous two days (above). Just back from this view point the righthand of 3 tracks is followed that winds its way up a ski run to le Cuchon, following a generally south-westerly course. Le Cuchon lies on the west ridge of la Petite Autane. On the far side of this ridge, the ski area and forest are left behind and the route follows a well graded stony path that at first heads eastwards, passing to the right of a hollow, before starting the gentle descent past shattered rock faces of the Autanes. This path twists and turns and at 1,690m splits. The left fork zigzags uphill, but our route continues to the right climbing briefly to a view point with a stone seat and a large cairn (below).

The stone seat with a view over the Rouanne Valley

From there the path zigzags down to a stony track which in turn leads to the rough road that heads down the valley towards Ancelle. This is followed westwards on the north side of the Rouanne Torrent. After a while a minor track to the left bypasses a long loop in the road before rejoining the road, which is then followed into Ancelle. This large village lies at the entrance to the Rouanne Valley. The Logis-Hotel les Autanes www.hotel-les-autanes.com is situated towards the west side of the village. This is a pleasant place to spend a night and it has a good restaurant, but is rather more up-market and expensive than most stopovers used on these walks. There is also a chambre d'haut/table d'haut on the east side of the village.

Day 4: Ancelle to Gîte des Trois Colls les Gourniers (1,477m)

16.1km, up 1,350m, down 1,200m, high point the Col de la Coupa 2,323m, 6h05 including the ascent of le Piolit:
22.7km, up 1,870m, down 1,720m, high point le Piolit 2,484m, 8h35

This long, but memorable, outing climbs to a high point the Piolit on the most southerly Écrins ridge. The Piolit is the pointed peak (arrowed) in the photo below that was taken during the descent on the previous afternoon. In poor conditions it is possible to reach les Gourniers, saving some 2h30, by taking a straight up and down route over the Col de la Coupa, the left-hand col in the photo below. This still involves a climb to 2,323m. The pretty hamlet of Les Gorniers is set in the Réallon valley, which drains south into the Durance. The Drac valley covered during the previous days' walks, by contrast, heads north to the Isère

The Piolit (arrowed) seen the previous day from just south of le Cuchon

After crossing the road bridge at the east end of the village the walk follows the broad stony track that runs eastwards along the southern bank of the Rouanne Torrent. Eventually, as the track turns down to cross the river, two narrower tracks leave to the right. The walk follows the righthand of these, signed to the Col de la Pourrachière. This track climbs steeply east-southeastwards and is followed to the left at a fork. At 1,732m another left fork leads eastwards and after a further 0.4km a right fork to the southeast goes out of forest and continues to climb across open hillside. At first this track makes its way round a cirque and then passes to the south of a bergerie. The route then follows a path heading north-eastwards. On reaching a rock face this path turns to the right and continues to climb below the cliff. At the end of the cliff the path zigzags eastwards up grassy slopes to the Col de la Pourrachière (2,173m and 8.5km from Ancelle). A well-made path, signposted to the Col de Chorges and le Piolit descends east-southeast from the col across grassy hillside. The IGN map indicates there is an alternative more direct route from the Col de la Pourrachière up the Bonaparre to the east ridge of the Piolit. This route, however, is not signposted at the col and there is no obvious path going up the Bonaparre. After a little under a km on the signed path, during which 90m height is lost, the path turns to the north and then northeast. It then joins a track and soon a signpost at 2,040m indicates a path leaving to the right towards the Col de Chorges (2.5km, 0h45) and the Piolit (3.4km, 1h20). The detour to the summit of the Piolit and back from here takes some 2h30.

A misty view south from the Col de la Coupa

On the return to the signpost the track is followed northeastwards for some 0.25km to a point where it winds sharply to the left. Just before this bend a well-made path leaves to the right, zigzagging up to the Col de la Coupa (above). The path on the descent from this col is way-marked with green circles on a white background. At first this is easy to follow as it zigzags down steep gritty gravel. When the gradient eases the path becomes indistinct as it crosses grassy hillside eastwards towards the Cabane du Vallon. To the right of the cabane the hillside drops away steeply. The way-marked route descends this steep section from a few metres past the cabane on an eroded gritty path, or rather series of eroded parallel paths, that lead down to more level grassy ground. The way-marks then continue to the left of the valley stream. Sometimes there is a path, but this is not well made and is frequently eroded. Eventually the way-marks direct the walker across the stream and this then is crossed twice more. The path becomes more certain after the second crossing to the right of the stream. Now the stream drops away to the left and the path continues through woodland. On reaching a stony track the route continues downhill to a metaled lane. This is followed to the left downhill through two loops to the hamlet of les Gourniers. The Gîte des Trois Cols www.gitedes3cols.fr/ lies to the left of the lane just before the centre of the hamlet. This large and popular gîte (below) has comfortable rooms with their own shower rooms and toilet. The lively communal meals are served in a large dining room.

Gîte des Trois Cols with the cone of the Pointe de la Diable in the background

Day 5: les Gourniers to Gîte d'Étape les Charançons (1,575m)
15.0km, up 1,448m down 1,339m high point Col de la Règue 2,706m, 6h08

The highest point on the whole walk is reached today. A few yards down the road from the gîte the route heads up a lane to the left. It passes a small stone chapel on the right and then joins a well-made path that climbs to the west of the Torrent de Réallon. This path heads northwards up the gorge of a valley, with high peaks on either side. The view ahead is dominated by the conical rock-face of the Pointe de la Diable seen in the background of the photo above. The path climbs to a ledge in the valley wall on its way to the small Chapelle St Marcelin. After this the route contours north-eastwards to a side stream where the main valley turns east. The path then climbs to the Cabane du Pré d'Antoni (1,850m) before dipping to the river and crossing alpine water meadows. Then the climb starts to the Cabane de Chargès at 2,206m. This ascent is steep in places, but is always on a good path that winds up the hill on the north side of the cascading Torrent de Chargès. The Cabane de Chargès is an active bergerie. From there the path becomes more ambiguous as there are multiple tracks made by grazing animals. It is important to find the maroon diamond-painted waymarks and cairns that indicate the way to the Col de la Règue. Initially the route climbs gradually just north of east across grass. Some 0.25km beyond the Cabane the route turns to the southeast and undulates over the high alpine meadowland for a further 0.8km. Then the way-marks follow a shallow grassy buttress, round to the east. After 0.1km the route turns to the north and the steep zigzagging climb to the col begins. At first this is mainly across grass, but in the last section the route climbs on moderately steep scree. The first section over the scree heads south-eastwards up to a point just below the ridge. Then the path turns to the left and after a couple of short zigzags follows a course northwards below the rocky ridge, before eventually reaching the breach in the rock wall that is the Col de la Règue.

The Vallon du Tissap from the Col de la Règue

There is a magnificent view from the col (above) looking east across the Vallon du Tissap to the rocky cliffs of the Tête du Tissap and on to the snow-capped Monte Viso and Chambeyron Hills on the skyline. The way-marked route in the last sections on either side of the col does not appear to be shown accurately on the IGN 1:25k map. It is recommended to follow the way-marks here and not rely on GPS.

The descent of the Vallon du Tissap, on the far side of the col, is to the northeast. As mentioned above, the well-placed way-marks on the first section should be followed rather than the map. These way-marks lead northeast for longer than is indicated on the map before they guide walkers to a safe way down the steep hillside to the Caban du Tissap. After passing to the right of this cabane and crossing the valley stream there is a clear path, which is in much better condition than that negotiated on the previous day's descent. It continues to the right of the stream, passing the Ancien Cabane du Tissap and then making the long descent through woodland high above the valley stream.

Gîte Auberge des Charançons

Eventually, after descending more than 1000m from the col, the path joins a track, with some buildings on the far side. This track is followed to the right as it climbs gently. Soon it joins a stony road that winds down 100m over 0.7km to the Gîte-Auberge des Charançons (above) gite-des-charancons.pagesperso-orange.fr/ . This pleasant gîte/restaurant, run by Martine and Alain Putoto, lies in the forest above the river at the base of the deep-sided, remote Rabioux valley. Again this river drains into the Durance in the south. Except in July and August the gîte is only open if a booking is made and a deposit paid. Alain is an excellent chef and good company, so you are in for a memorable evening meal. The gîte has comfortable dormitory accommodation. If the hot water system on the inside showers is not operating turn on the cold (blue) tap if you want a hot shower in the outside washroom.

Day 6: les Charançons to Prapic (1,562m)
14.8km, up 1,188m, down,1,128m, high point Col des Tourettes 2,582m, 5h37

There is a magnificent climb today up the steep south-facing slope to the dramatic twin pillars that mark the Col des Tourettes (below). The hillside during the ascent is a natural rock garden with an great variety of plants. Although the approach to the col is steep, the path throughout is well graded and maintains a comfortable angle.

The Col des Tourettes with the Crête de la Dent in the background

The route retraces the steps from the end of the previous day following the stony lane back to the buildings at 1,644m. From there a signposted path meanders across the valley floor through woodland and meadow to the valley stream-bed. The stream itself here frequently flows entirely underground. On the far side, the path heads in a general westerly direction, climbing through increasingly steep meadow. After going through the 2,000m contour the path turns and climbs steeply to the north and goes through several zigzags before reaching the col. This fine pass lies on the ridge between the Crête de la Dent and the Mourre Froid.

Beyond the col the path zigzags down to a high plateau, with two small lakes, which at the end of summer may be dry. The excellent path continues northwards along the lip of a hanging valley, with the cliffs of the Barre des Rougnous falling to the left. From here on a clear day one can look west to the distant Vieux Chaillol and the col crossed on the second day's walk (photograph page 175). After the path has worked round to the west it starts to descend to the basin below the cliffs. On reaching the lip of a lower hanging valley, la Barre de la Cabane, the path zigzags down grassy alp to the right of a stream to another valley floor at around 1,900m.

The Saut du Lairein in May

At the end of this hanging valley there is a footbridge bridge over a waterfall, the Saut du Lairein, on the infant River Drac Noir. This is a popular destination for people doing a day-walk from Prapic. The photo above looks back up the valley from below this waterfall during the ski touring season in May. From the waterfall the well-made and much-used track stays on the right side of the valley, winding down to the pretty, car-free village of Prapic,. The Gîte/Auberge Jabiore http://www.bienvenue-a-la-ferme.com/paca/hautes-alpes/orcieres/ferme/ferme-auberge-la-jabiore/266441 (+33 4 92 55 75 10) lies across the square from the church. Meals are taken in the Auberge, while comfortable bunk-room accommodation is provided in the gîte a short distance away. Again the restaurant and gîte are only open during the summer season, unless a prior booking is made.

Day 7: Prapic to les Borels (1,273m)
17.8km, up 724m, down 972m, high point le Giardet 1,650m, 5h

After the high passes of the previous days this walk takes a less-elevated route on the wooded south side of the Drac Noir. This avoids the sprawling ski resort above Orcières and provides a relatively gentle, but pleasant final day. The route largely reverses that done on day 8 in Chapter 2.

The walk starts by wandering the 3 km down the quiet road from Prapic to les Fourés. Here the route takes the lane that leads down to and across the river, before winding up through fields on the far side. A short way past the houses at les Chabauds our route turns left at a fork in the lane. After fording a stream a left turn is taken at a further fork. This heads steeply up a rough concrete-surfaced track that leads past the Chalet. Then a recently-made forestry track is followed that winds up through woods to le Girardet.

View down the Drac Noir Valley from above les Audiberts

Toward the end of this track the fields to the left give a magnificent floral display in early summer (photo page 19). The steep footpath shown on the IGN map that shortcuts long loops in this forestry track was still walkable in September 2016, but it is becoming overgrown through lack of use and may, in time, be lost. The forestry track ends in a clearing, where there is a signpost indicating a path that descends towards les Audiberts. This curves to the left while descending steeply to a track, where there are good views down the valley (above). This track is followed to the left to the village. After turning right down the lane the route goes through two hairpin bends before following a side lane to the left that becomes a broad forestry track. This traverses along the steep southern side of the Drac Noir valley, keeping some 200m above the river. It is pleasant walking through the forest with frequent views across the valley.

Eventually just before the Village of Serre Eyrauds our route again joins GR50. This comes along the track from the opposite direction and is followed as it makes a descent of the steep escarpment on a diagonal path that heads north-eastwards through beech wood. On reaching the river this is crossed by a long wooden footbridge, after which GR50 is followed westwards on a broad meandering track that runs parallel to the north bank of the river. Eventually the track joins up with the main valley road and this is briefly followed to the left before turning onto a leafy track on the far side of the road. After about a km this pleasant track meets up with the lane that runs up the east side of the Drac Blanc. It is possible to follow GR50 from here crossing the river and continuing along the path followed on the third day that traverses above the west bank of the river and leads to the bridge at les Borels. Alternatively, as it is quicker to head straight up the lane to the village, you may be tempted to do this to get an earlier celebratory drink at the excellent Auberge des Ecrins www.aubergedesecrins.com.

The Drac Blanc and les Borels from the Tour de Vieux Chaillol path on Day 1

9 APPENDICES

When to walk

The seasons when it is practical to undertake the different walks described in this book varies with the maximum height achieved and whether nights are spent in alpine huts. These refuges are normally only open between mid-June and mid-September. Although the second half of June and early July is a great time to be in the hills and the alpine flowers are at their best snow may be a problem on the higher routes. An ice axe and light instep crampons may provide sufficient protection in these circumstances, but on occasions these are not adequate and the route may need to be altered to avoid serious snow and ice climbing. The first two weeks in September has proved a good time to walk. The hills are less busy than in July and August and the walking conditions are often good in terms of temperature and absence of steep snow. Mid-July to mid-August provide good conditions, but overnight stopovers may be crowded and booking is essential.

Two of the walks can be undertaken from mid-May until the end of September. These are the traverses of the Cévennes and the Diois Hills circuit. The Dévoluy and Vercors walk would be good from early June. These 3 lower walks may well be uncomfortably hot in July and August.

Mapping

The French IGN maps are now available free on the French government website https://www.geoportail.gouv.fr/. All of the routes described in this guide have been updated to the October 2017 version of the Geoportail maps. The names of different footpaths and their course can vary with time. Where this makes a major difference to a route, as in the walk between Isola 2000 and Refuge Laus, it has been mentioned in the text.

IGN maps can also be purchased in electronic form from Ordinance Survey which enables you to use the Memory Map software and to load them on to portable GPS systems which can be a useful adjunct to a paper map and compass www.memory-map.co.uk/. The memory map software allows one to plot and calculate the length, ascent and descent of routes and print these.

After drawing the route I print this out at 1:25k double-sided on A4 paper. This saves a lot of weight compared with using the commercially-printed IGN maps.

Of course, 1:25k electronic maps of France can, also be obtained through IGN, but be warned the memory map and IGN software are not compatible, so all your maps should be purchased through one source or the other. The IGN maps I bought some years ago of the Ardech and Cevennes require the user to have a DVD in the computer. I suspect the IGN software may be less restrictive now.

Most of the GR paths in the French Alps are now shown, although not labelled, on Google Earth. Google Earth has a route drawing facility. When I have cross-checked this against Memory Map calculations the results of the two systems are remarkably comparable.

Estimated times for each day's walk

The estimated time for each day's walk is based upon the following formula:

> One hour for each 5 km walked plus 1 minute for each 10m ascent and 1 minute for each 30m descent.

In general this works well, but it will tend to underestimate walks over tricky ground and overestimate those where the route is on smooth paths. These estimates, therefore, must only be taken as a rough guide.

Finding and Booking accommodation

The accommodation we used on these walks is set out at the end of each day's account. In most cases the web site of the lodging is given, but where this is not available a telephone number or email address is provided. These web sites were all operational in August 2017. We have always booked accommodation in advance. This is particularly important at weekends when huts may be full. Even if the hut is not full booking gives the warden time to make sure food is in stock and may set alarm bells ringing if a party fails to arrive. When booking accommodation tell them where you are walking from so that they can phone up the previous night's lodging if you fail to show. In my experience the guardiens of huts are remarkably responsible at making these checks.

Sometimes it is necessary to pay a deposit, which is easy if a debit or credit card number is accepted. This is the case for many of the CAF huts and most, but not all hotels. Sometimes other lodgings ask for a cheque. I have always managed to persuade such lodgings that this is impracticable from the UK and offer to pay by bank transfer. Often they wave the deposit at this stage, but if they want a transfer this can be done from a British Bank to a European Bank for a fee of about £10. Although this is expensive for one person it is not too bad if you are a group of four walkers. The name and address of the account holder as well as those of the bank are required together with both the BIC and IBAN numbers of the recipient's account. Finally if you happen to be in France some time before your walking trip you can purchase a Mandat Cash (postal order) at a French post office and send this to secure a reservation.

Hopefully this guide will take the hard work out of finding accommodation, but if you want to find alternatives the first thing to do is to find a location where you want to obtain lodging using maps, or Google Earth. Then look for lodgings using the web. Ideally try and obtain the web site of the lodging itself. I try to avoid a booking agency unless it is used by the lodging place itself e.g. Logis de France.

Wherever possible try and get confirmation from the lodging by email and take a copy of this with you. It is then impossible for the lodging to say you have no booking. As I speak reasonable French I make my bookings in that language. Only a proportion of the lodgings speak English and in this case the reader may find it helpful to use Google Translate https://translate.google.co.uk/.

Most huts and many gîtes d'étapes will only accept payment in cash, so ensure you have sufficient Euros.

Equipment

Every walker will have their own equipment preferences, but it may be helpful to list the kit I take on a two week walk in the Alps.

1 rucksack 45-50L. This should give plenty of room for your kit. I use a 48 litre Osprey Kestrel.
1 waterproof rucksack liner
1 waterproof rucksack cover
I pair Gortex-lined mid-height light-weight walking boots
I pair of shoes for evenings I use GTX light-weight trainers, which can act as a back-up for boots if the former get waterlogged. Most of the walks described can be done in trainers.
3 pairs of cotton rich socks that will dry overnight after washing
2 light-weight quick-dry short-sleeved walking shirts
1 light-weight quick-dry long-sleeved shirt for travelling and the evenings
1 pair shorts; these are the usual attire for walking and in poor weather are a better base for waterproof overtousers.
1 pair long walking trousers for travelling and evenings
3 pairs quick-dry boxer shorts

1 light-weight microfleece jumper
1 light-weight Gortex shell top
1 pair light-weight Gortex shell trousers
1 thermal vest to sleep in and as an extra layer in emergencies
1 sun hat
1 pair photosensitive glasses or sun glasses
1 pair fleece gloves
1 fleece balaclava. You may never use this but it could be helpful in an emergency
1 light-weight quick-dry camping towel
1 light-weight cloth to cover hut pillows
1 silk sheet sleeping bag
1 light weight survival bag
1, 1 litre water bottle, in high summer you may need twice as much as this particularly at lower altitudes
1 LED light head torch with new batteries
1 sponge bag with 50ml toothpaste, tooth brush, bar soap (for washing clothes and yourself), nail brush (doubles as hair brush), plasters, nail scissors, ear plugs (bunk rooms can be noisy), a thin 3m clothes line, needle and thread, light weight pen knife.
High factor sun cream
Compass
Watch preferably with an altimeter
Pocket camera e.g Cannon Powershot S120, a spare memory card, a spare batteries so that you will not need to carry a charger.
Kindle; fully charged this should last a fortnight's walk
Mobile phone + charger and adaptor
Maps
Boarding passes
Record of Bookings
Train tickets
Wallet, Currency, health insurance card, Visa debit card, Mastercard
Passport
Route schedule
4 Small self-sealing polythene bags
1 A4 self-sealing map folder to store all the maps and papers
1 A5 self-sealing map folder for the day's maps
A small notebook and ball-point pen to keep a log
In late June consider taking an ice axe and instep crampons.
Many people find a pair of walking poles useful.
The above equipment should give you a packed rucksack, with the day's lunch that weighs comfortably under 9kg.

INDEX

Accommodation	194
Agence de Colombe	155
Aiguille(s)	
du Pertuis	19,22,176,177,178
Tortisse	162
de Chambeyron	165
Ancelle	176,**183**
Arvieux	167,170
Atlantic-Mediterranean watershed	57
l'Aubaret	65
Auberge	
des Allières	121,**125**
Buissonnière	120
de la Cure	29-30
du Desert	84
des Écrins	177,192
Jabiore	23
des Mures	138
l'Ocanière	21
la Petite	9,80,96
Provençal	146
Val Casterino	134
les Audiberts	23,191
Avèze	47,52-53
l'Aupillon	8,**13**,99,**110**
l'Authion	144,146,149
Baisse	
de l'Arpette	130
du Basto	128,130,135
de Camp d'Argent	144,**148**
Caveline	149
Baisse	
de la Combe	139
de la Déa	148
de Linière	147
Prals	132
de St Véran	149
de Valauretta	130,134
Balcon de Glandase	95
Banne	89,**92**
les Baraquements de Viraysse	164
la Barge	29
le Barral	51
Barre de la Cabane	190
Barre-des-Cévennes	59,**61**
Barre-des-Rougnous	190
le Barry	19, 20
Bas Gicons	17
la Bastide-Puylaurent	69,**75**
la Béal du Jas du Col	30
Bea Orchid	43
le Bec Roux	165
Bellecost	66
Belvedere de la Mourière	169
Bergerie	
des Ayes	11
de Chamoussel	117
du Jas Neuf	10
Roybon	124
les Bertrands	85
les Bonnets	21,179
Bonaparre	185
Bonneval	94

Boulc	89,94	les Charançons	176,188
Blandas	47	le Château	9
le Boréon	136,137,151	Château	
le Borie	71	d'Assas	51
les Borels	173,176,**177**,181,192	de Colombier	111
Brec de Chambeyron	165	de Passières	11
Breil-sur-Roya	144	Queyras	167,**169**
Briançon	6,28,**36**,167,**171**	Châtillon-en-Diois	8,79,89,**94-95**
Brunissard	170	le Cheylard	109
		Chemin	
Cabane		des Templiers	13,110
des Aiguillettes	120	de la Coupette	42
de Chargès	186	de l'Énergie	160-161
de Chaumailloux	10,118	de St Guilhem-le-Desert	45
du Chorum Clot	16,104	Chichilianne	8,11
du Col	30	Cime	
de l'Essaure	117	du Diable	144,149
des Pièrres	18	de la Gonella	148
du Pré d'Antoni	186	de la Palu	131
Pré Pourri	90	de Piagu	151,153
Sous le Rocher	166	du Pisset	130,137,153
de la Rama	103	de Prals	157
du Tissap	188	de Rause	149
du Vallon	186	de la Vallette de Prals	130,132
le Caïre Gros	130,139	du Ters	147
Can Noire	60	Circuit le Peyre Martin	45
Cap de Brion	58	Cirque de Sérrane	45
Cascade de la Pisse	181	Cirque des Navacelles	49,51
Casterino	130,134	le Clappier	22
les Cayres	71	Côtes de Venasque	181
le Cayla	59,63	Col	
Cazilhac	37,40	des Abeilles	63
Ceillac	27,28,167,169	Agnel	31
Cévennes	37-76	des Aiguilles (Dévoluy)	99,**101**
les Chabauds	23,191	des Aiguilles (Glandage)	111
Chaillol	19,21	de l'Aupet	119
Chaillol 1600	21	des Ayes	167,**170**
Chalet	191	du Barn	130,138
Chalets des Ayes	23,170	de Beaufayn	81
Chalets de Vers le Col	170	du Berceau	144,**145**
la Chalp	167,**170**	de la Blache	20
Chambres/Tables d'Hôte		du Buisson	79,85
Ammonite, Mas Guillou	49	de Cabre	89,**93**
Château le Colombier	111	du Caille	87
la Source	89,**92**	de Carabes	91
Champoléon	173	des Caux	79,95
Chapelas Roc	68	de Cendri	20
Chapelle Ste-Anne	29	de Chamauche	85
Chapelle St Marcelin	186	de Chamoussier	28,31

Col
- de Charnier 14-16,99,104-105
- du Charron 89,91
- de Chorges 185
- de Clemens 176,180-181
- des Combes 89,91
- de Côte Chèvre 115,**116**
- de la Coupa 176,**185**
- de Croix 16,105
- des Deux 122
- de l'Escallier 20
- des Faisses 60
- de Fer 162
- du Festre 102
- de Fond Sauvage 87
- du Fort 130,140
- de Freissinières 19,**24**
- Fromage 167,**169**
- de la Guercha 157
- de Girardin 28,29
- de Greuson 117
- de Jalcrest 63
- de Jargène 108
- de Jiboui 113
- de Larch 164
- des Laupies 62
- du Lausfer 151,**156**
- de Lauzeto 91
- des Lièvres 79,85
- de la Lombarde 151,155
- de Lus 8,**13**,99,**100**
- de Mallemort 159,164
- Malrif 34
- Martin 79,85
- Marquairès 60
- de la Maure 79,86
- de Menée 8,**11-12**,113
- de Mercière 154
- Navite 13,110
- de la Noir 28,30
- de Noyer 18
- du Pison 10
- Pouriac 163
- de Pourrachière 184-185
- du Prayet 8,11
- des Prêtres 13,110
- de Raisis 28,34
- de Raus 149
- de Razet 146

Col
- de la Règue 176,**187**
- du Roi 89,93
- du Royet 79,82
- de Saboulé 151,156
- de Salèse 130,138,151,154
- Salidès 60
- St Pierre 88
- Serenne 159,**166**
- Seysse 12
- la Saume 15,**17**
- des Tourettes 176,189
- des Thures 33
- de Valdrôme 93
- de Veillos 138
- Vert 121,**124**
- Vieux 28,32
- Voraire 139
- le Cuchon 176,**182**

Coulet de Pécoval 74
Colla Bassa 144,146
Collette
- de Gilly 33
- de Tortisse 162
- des Trous 140

Combe
- la Mayt 17
- des Natges 45
- Noire 94

Crête
- Crête des Babarottes 159,**161**
- de la Dent 189
- de Gilly 28,**33**
- de Jiboui 99,113
- de la Mourière 168-169
- de la Taillante 32

Croix
- de Berthel 65
- de Justin 79,**80**

Daffodils (wild) 57
les Deux Sœurs 124
Dévoluy 5,14-18,97-108
Die 5,8,**9**,**77**,79,**80**,**96**
le Dôme 8,79
Dormillouse 19,**25**
le Duffre 91

Ecogîte de Valjouvès 63

Écrins	5,18-26,173-192	Gîte d'Étape	
Elderflower orchid	38	le Ranquas	40,**46**,47
Equipment	195	Relais des Merveilles	130,**132**,152
Eygliers	26	le Rocher Rond	103
		le Tarsimoure	88
Ferm		Glandage	89,99,**111**
des Chazaux	8,9	Gorges	
du Désert	114	de la Bourne	73
de Esparron	11	de Büech	100
la Chastre	17	de Toussière	109
les Ferriers	94	de la Vis	46-51
les Fonts	28,34	les Gourniers	176,186
les Fourés	23,191	la Grande Autanne	176
Fouillouse	159,**165**	la Grande Mucherolle	121
Freissinières	26	la Grande Sœur Agatha	123
		Grand Ferrand	15,99,104
Ganges	40	Grand Glaiza	34
Genolhac	64	Grande Randonnée (GR)	
Gillestre	19,**26**,28	4	71-72
Girardet	19,23,176,191	5	27,29,36,139-140,158,
Gîte			163-164,165, 169-171
du Boréon	137,153	7	48-53,57-63,65-66
le Chamois	179	9	126
des Charançons	188	50	20-22,26,177-180,191-192
de la Cure	29	52	135-138,145-150,154
du Combau	117	52a	131
Dévoluy	17	58: Tour du Queyras	31-33
d'Ecole	25	58 variante	33
les Granges	165	60	55
Jabiore	23,190	60A	53-55
la Sauvagine	13	62C	55
des Trois Cols	186	72	65-68,73
Gîte d'Étape		74	45
d'Air de Côte	54,**58**,59	91	124-126
les Baladins	169	91 variante	93
Cap de Côte	54,55	91/93	10
le Cassu	33	93	16-18,104-108,113
le Chalet Viso	170	93 & 93 variante	12,14,16,17
de Chatillon	95	94	100-102,109
le Corborant	158	95	80-83,94-96
le Croisette	61	653D	26
l'Estive du Mercantour	148	GR du Pays (GRP): Tour	
Ferm de St Antoin	79,**86**	de Chassezac	68
des Gondoins	19,22	du Font Sancte	27,168-169
Grand Traversée des Alps	164	du Larzac Méridional	45-48,50
la Jarjatte-Valgabondage	14	de Montagne Ardèchois	73
de Loubaresse	72	de Vieux Chaillol	178
Mas de la Barque	64,**67**	Grand Surnom	87
le Pilhon	93	Grand Veymont	10,115,117,**120**,122

les Grands Deux	122
Grenoble Gare Routière	100,121,126
Gresse en Vercors	115,**120**,121
Grimone	8,13
Guillestre	25-28
Haute Bouffet	14,101
l'Hospitalet	59,60
Hotel	
les Autanes	183
les Bruyères	55
Cantinat-fleuri	27
le Commerce (Lus)	100,108
du Commerce (le Vegan)	53
au Gai Soleil de Mt Aiguille	118
Gorges de Chassezac	69
la Neyerette	16
le Mt Barral	115
les Norias	40
Mas de Luzière	40,**42**
Infornas Hauts	20
Isola 2000	151,**154**
la Jarjatte	8,**14**,100
le Jocou	8,**12**
Lac(s)	
d'Agnel	163
du Basto	135
di Colle di Santa Anna	155,156
Égorgéou	32
de Colle Longue	158
de Derrière-la-Croix	163
du Diable	150
Foréant	32
Fourca	150
Grand Lac des Esteris	24
Gros	138
Lausfer	156
Lauzanier	164
du Lauzon	105
Millefonts	138
Miroir	27
de la Muta	150
de la Noire (Quéras)	30
Noir (Mercantour)	135
des Pisses	24
de Roue	170

Lac(s)	
Ste-Anne	29
Saorgine	133
Trem	150
du Vallonnet Superior	165
Vert	135
Lachaup	99,**103**
Larche	159,164
Lubaresse	69,72
Luc en Diois	79
Lus-la-Croix-Haute	8,14,99,**100**,108
Madières aqueduct	48
la Madone de Fenestre	137,151,**152**
les Maillefauds	111
les Maisons	170
Maljasset	28,29
Mangiabo	144,148
Maouné	144
Mapping	193
les Marrons	21,176,**179**
Mas du Pont	48
Menton Garvan	144,145
Mercantour	130-140,147-155,160-164
la Meyrie	14
Mère Eglise	16,17
Military orchid	51-52
Mont	
Aigoual	54,**56-58**
Aiguille	10,115,117,**119**
Barral	8,**12**,99,**113**
Chalancha	139
Clappier	135
Giagiabella	146
Lozère	64-68
Mont Mounier	156
Tournairet	140
Montagne	
de l'Aup	90
de Beaufayn	79,81
du Bouges	65
de France	99
de St Gicon	17
de Label	95
de Longue Serre	86
de Paille	99,107
de Tarsimoure	79,**87-89**,92
la Monta	32
Montdardier	40,47,52

Mont-Dauphin	26
Monte Viso	5,24,31,32,34,155,162,187
Montlahuc	79,87
Montpellier	40
Montselgues	69,71
la Motte-Chalancon	79,86
Moucherotte	121,**126**
Moulins de la Foux	49-50
le Mourre Froid	176,189
Mur des Aîttes	35
Navacelles Hamlet	48,49
les Nonnières	99,**114**,115
Notra Dame des Neiges	74
Occitainie	37
Orcières	23
Pallon	26
Pan de Sucre	31
Pas	
de l'Aiguille	115,118
de l'Arpette	130,133,150,151
de Bachassons	120
de Bœuf	142,151,**157**
de Bret	79,**96**
de Cavale	159,162-163
de Colle Longue	158
du Corbeau	81
de la Couletta	159,**165**
du Diable	144,149,**150**
du Loup	81,84
du Mont Colomb	130,136
de Morgan	159,162
de la Roch	95
des Roubines de la Maïris	137
de Ste Anne	156
de la Selle	120
Peonies (wild)	87
le Pertus	139
la Petite Autane	182
les Petits Deux	122
Petit Paris	71
Pennes-le-Sec	79,83
Peyre Moutte	28,35
Peyre Martine	40,44-45
Pied-de-Borne	64,**68-70**
Pied-du-Mélezet	27,28
Pierre Blanche	121

Pic(s)	
de Barette	34-55
de Bure	15
Cassini	64
d'Escreins	167,**168**
du Malrif	28,34
de la Font Sancte	168
le Pilhon	89,**93**
le Piolit	176,184,185
Plan	
de Fontmort	61
du Lyon	145
Pointe de la Diablé	176,186
Pointe de Ventabren	148
Points des Estaris	19
le Pont	70
Pont	
Countet	133,152
Hérault	54
d'Ingolf	154
de Montvert	64
du Samoust	27
les Poranches	21
les Poujols	50
Puech Pointu	41
Pradelle	79,84
Prapic	19,**23**,176,**190**
Pré la Chaup	18
Pré de la Font	115,117
Pré Premier	170
la Pyramide	89,91
Queyras	5,27-36,166-171
Ravel	79,89,**94**
la Ravolt	112
Refuge	
Agnel	28,**31**
Basse Roua	159,**166**,167
de Cervières	34
de Chambeyron	165
de Fontanalba	134
Madone de Fenestre	137,**152**
des Merveilles	133,144,**150**,151
la Monta	32
de Nice	130,**136**
de la Soldanelle	121,**123-124**
la Tour de Berg	113
de Tourond	181

Refuge	
de Valmasque	134-135
Vens	159,**161**
Régos	47
Richardière	11,115,**118**
les Richards	21,178
les Ricous	182
Rifugio Lause	151,**157**
Rimon	79,**82**
Riou Mort	21
River	
Altier	64,68,
l'Arre	47,53,54
Bévéra	147
Borne	70,73
Buëch	5,14,97,99,100
Buèges	40,43-44
Chassezac	69,70
Drac	5,15,17-19,21,176,177
Drac Blanc	21,22
Drac Noir	21-23,190,191,192
Drôme	8,79,80,89,92
Durance	6,19,26,184
Guil	19,26-28,32,169
Hérault	37,40,54,55
Roanne	84
Roya	127
Tarn	57,64,66
Tarnon	59,60
Tinnée	127,158
Ubaye	30,166
Ubayette	164
Vérié	66
Véssubie	127
Vis	37,46-50
Roc Roux	15
Roc Blanc	40-42
Roche(s)	
Courbe	16,104
Du Saboulé	157
Rousse	24
Rocher(s)	
du Baux	82
de Blaches	79,83
du Caylaret	45
de Combau	116
du Marquis	47
de la Tude	47

le Rouve Bas	63
le Roux	28,**33**
les Roranches	179
Ruisseau see Stream	
les Salces	68
St Andéol	121,123
St-André-de-Buèges	40-42
St-André-de-Valborgne	59
St-Bonnet en Champsaur	5,15,18,19
St Crépin	19,26
St Dalmas	130,**138-139**
St Disdier	15-17
St-Étienne-de-Tinnée	151,158-160
St-Étienne en Dévoluy	15
St Grat	132
St-Jean-de-Buèges	40,41,44
St-Laurent-les-Bains	69,74-75
St-Martin-Vésubie	127,130,131,140
St-Maurice-Navacelles	47-48
St-Nazaire le Desert	79,**84**
St-Nizier-du-Mucherotte	121,**126**
St-Pierre-d'Argençon	89,92
Ste-Marguerite la Figure	70
San Bernolfo	157
Saut du Lairein	190
Sentier des Quatre Mille Marches	56
la Séranne	40-42
Serre	
Chauvière	82
du Charron	91
de l'Estelle	71
Serre-Eyrauds	22,191
Signal de Ventelon	64-65
Sommet de la Felgère	74
Sommet d'Espervelouze	75
Stream/Torrent/Ruisseau	
Berrièves	123
de Blaisil	23
du Boréon	138
de Chargès	186
des Combes	123
du Lac du Col	24
de la Montette	33
l'Unel	109
Rouanne	183-184
de Réallon	186

Mountains of the Provençal Rim

Sospel	144,146
les Sucettes de Borne	112
Taravel	93
Télésège du Gnourou	24
Tête	
de l'Adrech d'en Barris	155
de la Garnisier	14
de Lauzon	16,105
Mercière	151,154
de la Plainie	14
de Plate Lombarde	165
Rougnous	157
de Tissap	187
de Toillies	31
Vachères	15,101
Timing of Walks	194
Torrent see Stream	
Trois Becs	78,82,102
Tulips (wild)	62
Vacherie de Murans	140
Valance	5,9
Valleraugue	54,**55**
Valdrôme	88,89
Valley/Val/Vallée/Vallon/Vallone	
des Aiguilles	102
du Barn	138
Berrièves	122
Borne	70
Bouchouse	32
Escreins	166
Charnier	16,104
du Châtelet	166

Valley/Val/Vallée/Vallon/Vallone	
di Collalunga	158
Combau	117
Drobie	72
Drôme	8,77,79,89
Empuonrame	133,152
Fontanalba	134
Fourane	164
Freissinières	24-26
della Guerchia	157
du Lauzanier	163
Laugier	166
de la Miinière	133
des Pelouses	168
Rouanne	183
della Sauma	157
Tarnon	60
Tinnée	160
Tissap	188
Tourond	181
Ubaye	166
Valmasque	134
Veiljouvès-Bas	59,163
Venanson	140
Vercors	8-14
Plateau	5,8-10,117-118,120,124-126
eastern escarpment	12-14,110-126
le Vernet	179
Vieux Chaillol	19,20,175,180-181
le Vigan	47,**53**,54
Villefort	64,**68**
Viollins	25,26
When to walk	193

ABOUT THE AUTHOR

Ian MacLennan was born in the Scottish Highlands in 1939 and was introduced to walking in the hills at an early age by his mother. They moved south to Surrey in 1945 after his mother was widowed. He attended Guy's Hospital Medical School, where he joined the climbing club and started alpine climbing. After qualifying in medicine in 1964 he subsequently specialised in academic clinical immunology. After 10 years running a research group in the Nuffield Department of Clinical Medicine in Oxford he moved to the University of Birmingham in 1979. There he headed Immunology and the Medical Research Council Centre for Immune Regulation until his retirement from clinical work and administration in 2005. Since retiring he has been able to focus on immunological research and long walks in the hills. In Birmingham he became a member of the Birmingham Medical Research Expeditionary Society. This has enabled him to visit the Alps, Andes, Himalaya and Mountains of East Africa with like-minded friends, who have a passion for the high hills and an interest in altitude medicine. His wife, two sons and seven grandchildren all enjoy walking in the Hills.

Made in the USA
San Bernardino, CA
30 December 2017